**Praise for Joanne Holbr**

"What an incredible storyteller! Joanne provides enjoyable and adventurous stories with such insightful perspectives for parents, caregivers, guardians, etc. I appreciated the 'Lessons Learned' sections at the end of each chapter. I kept finding myself rereading them to reflect on their meaningful insights. As a parent of a daughter with Down syndrome, Chapter 6: Acknowledging Children with Special Needs and Their Parents, addresses possible ways for our world to become more inclusive. Bravo to Joanne for capturing how to enjoy and relish the honor of being a parent."

— **Bernadette Miller, Mother, Virginia, USA**

"In *Your Passport to Parenting*, Holbrook challenges our fears about raising our children and pulls from the wisdom of parents and cultures across the globe to share lessons in child rearing. Parents of children of all ages will reap the benefit of Holbrook's experience, engage on an adventure of parenting across cultures, and come away with a deep appreciation and desire to share the world with their kids."

— **Dr. Anna Fitch Courie, Mother, and Author of *The Adventures of Cancer Girl and God*, South Carolina, USA**

"Joanne took me on a journey around the globe, and on the way, she taught me that being a parent is about learning and making mistakes. Her insightful words filled with love and kindness and her teachings through storytelling made me realize I am not alone—all around the globe, women face the same challenges. There are moments when she asks you to stop, think, feel, and learn through your own experiences. Thank you for this all-encompassing adventure through parenting."

— **Olga Rosenburg, Business Owner, Mother, Sweden**

"Joanne captures the joys of parenting through personalized story-telling—taking the reader on a journey around the world, sharing memories, tips, and life lessons from parents far and wide. I hope there is as much fun and adventure in our family's future as there clearly has been in Joanne's."

— **Diane Sequeria, Project Manager, Mother, London, UK**

"Like a good jigsaw puzzle, Joanne distils wisdom from around the world to weave a compelling guide for parents. The stories in each chapter gently lead the reader to explore the many ways different cultures raise resilient offspring who can become friends with one another and share your core values. Joanne highlights many fine human qualities, including curiosity, compassion, and kindness. She persuasively presents the merits of open communication and clear and consistent boundaries to build a sound framework for happy, beautiful children."

— **Harry Armytage, The Learning Difficulty Expert™, Father, Canberra, Australia**

"*Your Passport to Parenting* is *the book* every parent should read who is searching for a different idea or a better way. Joanne offers a positive approach, with forethought and intention, that takes advantage of her incredible travel experiences. The stories are thought-provoking and force you to pause and ask yourself several questions about your own methods, traditions, and approaches. Some concepts reinforced what I've been doing as a parent while others gave me new ideas and techniques to try with my children. Joanne's approach for how I could speak to my daughter about the transition into womanhood utterly changed my life! This approach was exactly what I was searching for. If this book could reach every parent, it could very well change the world, one family at a time."

— **Melissa Venable, CEO, Mother, Virginia, USA**

"A book that packs a real parenting punch, *Your Passport to Parenting* has so many *aha!* moments that I couldn't help sharing with friends, and when I did, my friends exclaimed, "That's so brilliant! Mind if I use it myself?" So, if this book goes viral, it's really no surprise! It's an extremely fun and practical read that will inspire you, top off your parenting toolkit, and most certainly bless your family."

— **Candice Parsons, Writer and Communications Specialist, Mother, Perth, Australia**

"*Your Passport to Parenting* is such a breath of fresh air among parenting books. Rather than offering clinical, cold formulas for cookie-cutter parenting, it's full of relatable, sage anecdotes from around the world about every stage of child development, and it's applicable to any parenting style. In short, it's a collection of the best advice you've ever heard, wrapped into one source! I also appreciated the workbook format that lets you notate your personal connections to the material so you can easily recall them later, and the 'Lessons Learned' sections at the end of each chapter help summarize key points for later skimming and reference."

— **Alina Rozanski, Middle School Teacher, Mother, Bavaria, Germany**

"As a new parent, I found *Your Passport to Parenting* to be a friendly guide, full of original information. Parenting can be overwhelming, so I was beyond thrilled to find such an easy-to-read, idea-packed book. This book has my utmost recommendation. I read it on a film set, in between intense filming, and I can assure you it reads like a dear friend. I can't wait to share it with more parents."

— **Youssef Kerkour, Actor, Father, London, UK**

"As a mom of two boys (one being non-verbal and in a wheelchair and the other neuro-typical), I have read countless parenting books, many of which contradict each other and have left me doubting myself and feeling inadequate as a parent. *Your Passport to Parenting* is proof of the old saying: 'It takes a village to raise a child.' It has definitely made me slow down, breathe, and enjoy this incredible journey of parenting by being present for my children every day. Thank you for the inspiration to keep pushing on, Joanne."

— **Twone Moreland, Business Owner and Mother, Bali, Indonesia**

"I have read a lot of parenting books, but this one is different. Holbrook gives parents the framework to feel comfortable and confident in their parenting while building lifelong bonds with their children. She takes the reader on a journey through all the best family and parenting practices she has witnessed through her extensive exposure to many different cultures. There are many pearls of wisdom in these pages. So, so good."

— **Patricia Falcetta, The Family Joy Expert (TM), Mother, Canberra, Australia**

"In *Your Passport to Parenting*, not only will you learn international tools to help you become a stellar parent, but you'll be helping your children learn how to create their own destinies by becoming secure, well-adjusted, and successful future adults. You'll be amazed by the worldwide wisdom Joanne Holbrook provides here and be eager to apply it to your own family."

— **Patrick Snow, Father, Publishing Coach, and International Bestselling Author of *Creating Your Own Destiny* and *Boy Entrepreneur*, Hawaii, USA**

"Joanne Holbrook has provided what every other parenting book has long overlooked: that many ways exist to be a good parent, and just because you do things differently, doesn't mean you are doing them wrong. In *Your Passport to Parenting*, she provides tips from around the world about how to raise happy, well-behaved children without having to try to keep up with other parents. This is a breath of fresh air among parenting books."

— **Tyler R. Tichelaar, PhD and Award-Winning Author of** *When Teddy Came to Town*, **Michigan, USA**

"This powerful and dynamic book is chock-full of stories and activities from around the world and a must-have for any parent interested in conscientious parenting. It guides you to develop a proactive plan for teaching your children the values to form a strong moral foundation for their life's journey."

— **Susan Friedmann, CPA and Bestselling Author of** *Riches in Niches: How to Make it BIG in a Small Market*, **New York, USA**

THERE IS MORE THAN ONE WAY TO BE A GOOD PARENT

# YOUR PASSPORT TO PARENTING

## WISDOM FROM AROUND THE WORLD TO HELP BUILD HAPPY FAMILIES

## JOANNE HOLBROOK

AVIVA
PUBLISHING
New York

**Your Passport to Parenting: Wisdom from Around the World to Help Build Happy Families**

Published by:
Aviva Publishing
Lake Placid, NY
(518) 523-1320
www.AvivaPubs.com

Joanne Holbrook
joanne@yourpassporttoparenting.com

ISBN: 978-1-950241-77-4
Library of Congress Control Number: 9781950241774

Editors: Larry Alexander and Tyler Tichelaar, Superior Book Productions
Cover Design and Interior Book Layout: Nicole Gabriel, Angel Dog Productions
Author Photo: Peter Driessel Photography

Every attempt has been made to properly source all quotes.
Printed in the United States of America

Dedicated to every parent around the world.

# ACKNOWLEDGMENTS

I am blessed to have a tribe of people who have loved me for years and helped me through the process of writing and printing this book. In no particular order, thanks are due to:

My amazing husband, Deric, who saw this book in me long before I did. Thank you for enjoying this process with me every step of the way and always believing in me. I love you.

My children Kailey and Devin. Without you, this book and journey would never have happened. Thank you for choosing me; you are my heartbeat and my lungs. You both gave me the biggest gift I have ever been given—being your mom.

My dad, my biggest fan and biggest critic. Thank you for the fire. You were the one who taught me that the beauty in another person is in their story, and you were right.

My mom. Thank you for your continual love and support that helped me become the woman I am today. Thank you for always answering the phone.

Patrick Snow, my writing and publishing coach, who locked arms with me and was there for me through this whole process. Without your incredible guidance, this book would not be here.

My entire writing support team: Nicole Gabriel, Tyler Tichelaar, Larry Alexander, and Susan Friedmann. Your professional coaching, editing, designing, and publishing efforts have brought *Your Passport to Parenting* to life and were instrumental in its overall success.

Claudia, Diane, Wendy, and Mary, thank you for your continual support. You all have left your fingerprints all over this book, and it is better because of you.

Everyone who spoke to me, had coffee with me, and left me with the gift of their story or advice—I treasure you all.

# CONTENTS

# AN INTERNATIONAL JOURNEY THROUGH PARENTING

*"Perfect parents exist…but they don't have kids yet."*

*— Unknown*

Allow me to assume you are busy and in a hurry; of course you are; you are a parent. Even reading a book is a commitment you may have to think twice about (when on earth will you get time to read a whole book?), but I also know you understand your role in your child's development is the most important role you will ever have. If you are concerned about your child's development, and that you may be doing too much or too little, then you are like most other parents around the world. I understand completely and know where you are coming from because I am currently in your shoes sharing these same thoughts for my own children.

*Your Passport to Parenting* is going to give you international parenting viewpoints and concepts to help save you time, energy, and frustration. Each chapter covers topics you may be struggling with now or do not even know you will have to deal with yet, and nearly every page is filled with parenting inspiration and insights from around the world. My purpose is to provide thought-provoking ideas about values-based parenting for every age of childhood development to help you navigate your way through the parenting journey, using entertaining stories, lessons, ideas, and worksheets.

The greatest fear I hear parents express is: "What if I don't do this right?" Although our parenting instincts are meant to kick in when a child is brought into our lives, the truth is we still lie awake at night wondering how to deal with certain behaviors, situations, or maybe a lack of connection with our child that we crave. We pray we do not mess up our children and this most important task, parenting.

So, what do we do? We ask others!

*Your Passport to Parenting* provides you with proven concepts from other parents who have wisdom to share. Instead of only raising your children the way you were brought up, it gives you insight into how other parents around the world have raised their children, thereby allowing you to bring in multiple international parenting philosophies and design your own way of parenting using proven and successful methods.

One of my most prevalent realizations, and a main driver behind writing this book, was that not all parents enjoy parenting. This epiphany came to me when one of my best friends who does not have children said to me, "Why would anyone want kids? All parents do is complain about having them?" Her words made me step back to assess myself. I started listening to how parents speak about their parenting experiences. I noticed it is normal for parents to complain or say, "I need a bottle of wine at night," or "I just want to hide from them for a few hours." As a parent, I know these comments come out when we are overwhelmed. I also know every parent loves their children immensely. I decided then and there to have as much fun being a parent as my kids were having being children, and to find other parents who enjoyed parenting.

Thankfully, my life allowed me to experience different ways to parent from around the world. I started asking experienced moms and dads from different mindsets, marital situations, or cultures for their thoughts on parenting. What I found were literal gems: beautiful words of wisdom, life lessons, and stories from around the world. Learning these lessons and applying them to my life helped me fall in love with every aspect of parenting. Now when I have a glass of wine at night, it is because I want one, not because I need one.

Born in 1976, I grew up in South Africa during a terrible time in the country's history: the Apartheid (separation). The government controlled every aspect of the population, separating the country by race and tribe into different living areas. Being a privileged white child in a nation where we were not allowed to speak to anyone who was not "like us," I started to develop a singular life view. Nearly the entire world sanctioned South Africa in some manner. The government did not even allow TV to be broadcast until 1976 because it sought to regulate and control every bit of information coming into South Africa. Growing up in this incredibly controlled and segregated environment, I began noticing I was not living in a kind or connected place. Not until 1994, when Nelson Mandela became President and the Apartheid government was abolished, were we finally free from segregation. Then I vowed to learn as much as I could about other cultures in my own country and around the world. I wanted to learn everything I could about the people and cultures I had been restricted from knowing my entire life. I started to travel and learn more about how others around the world live.

Every place I have lived since leaving South Africa at age twenty-six has been a completely new cultural experience for me. My first cultural change was moving to England. I met my husband, a US Army Officer named Deric, in London. His job required him to move all over the world every two to three years. So, the changes and new experiences kept coming as we moved to new countries and learned completely new cultures. Our family has experienced eight international moves (so far). We have lived in five different countries and five different American states over the past fifteen years. And, as you do when living abroad, we have traveled and vacationed in dozens of countries. We've done all this while raising two active children, Kailey and Devin.

When you move so often and experience so much change, you always feel at a loss, like everyone knows and understands more than you do. So, the best way I could quickly empower myself at each new location was to ask questions about everything, including parenting. Each time I moved and learned a new culture, I could feel and see how each country had different rules, customs, and ways of parenting.

I want to share with you the wisdom, ideas, and parenting concepts I have gathered from all over the world simply because they are too fantastic not to share. Since I have experienced so many different cultures, I can act as a facilitator to help you see parenting from a different perspective. Sometimes if we are even just a little set in our ways, it is difficult to see another's way of parenting with an open mind. My background has allowed me to look at parenting problems and issues from multiple cultures. If you are given numerous good options as a parent, you automatically feel more empowered, and that is what *Your Passport to Parenting* can provide you: more options, more empowerment, and more understanding.

This is not a how-to parenting book. It is a conceptual parenting book, filled with ideas taken from parents around the world, consolidated in one place to help you. With these global parenting ideas, you may find a new outlook on how to raise your children to be strong, independent, and empathetic adults. You might find that parenting can actually be positive, calm, and enjoyable. Building a special bond with our toddler, young child, and then teenager is something we do not often take the time to think about holistically. But when we do, as you will learn to do in this book, the rewards can be endless. Our children are usually only dependent on us and available to receive our daily influence for about eighteen years, and that is if they are listening to us the entire time. After that, they are meant to fly away and start their own lives, trusting that we have given them all they need.

Are you ready to learn how others parent around the world? Do you want more options as a parent? Do you want to be a happier, better mother or father? Then grab a cup of tea, coffee, or your favorite drink, and meet me at the next chapter. Come with an open mind and a loving heart, and prepare yourself to see how others raise their families happily around the world.

Let's begin.

*Joanne Holbrook*

CHAPTER 1

# PARENTING INSIGHTS FROM SOUTH AFRICA

*"To be the father of a nation is a great honor, but to be the father of a family is a greater joy."*

— *Nelson Mandela*

Describing South Africa is difficult. Without giving a history lesson, let me give you a few facts for perspective. South Africa has eleven official languages. How the government keeps track of them, I will never know. The official languages are: Northern Sotho, Southern Sotho, Tswana, Swati, Ndebele, Xhosa, Zulu, Afrikaans, English, Venda, and Tsonga. Many unofficial languages are spoken in South Africa on top of the official eleven official languages, and every language has a different culture attached to it, with its own rituals, celebrations, beliefs, and ceremonies.

Nelson Mandela described this beautiful country as a rainbow nation, and you can see why. There is color everywhere—in the people, fabrics, landscape, language, and culture—creating a tangible vibration. This incredibly diverse country has beautiful lessons to offer the rest of the world.

I lived in South Africa for twenty-six years before I moved to England. The decision to leave was driven by my need for adventure, a calling I had heard all my life, not because I did not love South Africa, its beauty, or amazing cultures. Once you feel the vibration of Africa, you will always crave it, as I still crave it today.

## SOMETHING'S NOT QUITE RIGHT HERE

From 1947-1994, South Africans were divided into racial classifications. Your classification determined where you could live, whom you could marry, and where you could work. Every aspect of your life was controlled. Races were not allowed to mix in any manner whatsoever—unless, of course, the Apartheid government allowed non-whites to serve whites. Apartheid is a time that will haunt South Africa's history for generations.

As a child born in the mid-seventies, I was raised in a completely homogenous community. I was brought up as a privileged white child in South Africa during the Apartheid. It was something I did not understand, but I had no outside reference to go on; it was the only life I knew. The government kept people who were "not like us" away from the white population. What this actually meant was that I only saw, spoke to, or heard from people who were like me. Everyone was white and spoke English.

The government controlled everything the entire country heard and learned. It is difficult for many people to understand living in a state where everything you know has been censored. The government controlled the newspapers, TV news, and radio stations, and it censored every television show and every lesson taught in school. Since we were under sanctions, and there was no internet then, South Africans saw very little of the world. It was not possible as an elementary school child to know how to see further than what you learned in school. When you have nothing to compare a situation to, you do not compare it; you accept it. However, I do remember a day when my heart felt something was not quite right.

When my family went to church in the 1980s, blacks and whites were required to sit separately. But outside, there was no real way to separate the races. So naturally, when the children played outside after church, we all played together, and because children do not see or care about race, I made a friend. Her name was Thandi; she was a Zulu child. We would play each week outside the church building while the adults socialized after the service.

One day, I asked my dad if Thandi could come home with us so we could continue our game. My dad did not approve of Apartheid or the government. He taught me to learn a person's story before assuming you know them or judging them. He always said the Apartheid stole relationships and friendships from all South Africans.

But when I asked if Thandi could come with us, my dad looked at me, disappointment and sadness in his eyes, and said in a soft voice, "It is not possible for her to come play."

I looked over and saw Thandi asking her father the same question. Our fathers' eyes met, and they smiled sadly at one another. My dad nodded to him in respect; Thandi's dad nodded in return.

I never asked if she could play again.

I did not know what had happened, but I knew something was not quite right about it. I grasped that Thandi was not allowed to come to our house and play, but because segregation was not explained to me, I did not understand what was going on. Parents did not discuss these things with children in those days.

Not being allowed to speak to everyone was limiting and confining. I decided when I had kids, I would expose them to as many different people as I could—all cultures, colors, races, and religions. I wanted my children to see people and not feel that there was an "us" and a "them."

When it came to parenting, I adopted the attitude that we are all human. I wanted my kids to be able to play with anyone. When he was five, my son asked me what the difference was between a person with pink skin and a person with brown skin. Thinking of Thandi and all the lost relationships, I answered, "A person with pink skin's ancestors come from cold countries, and a person with brown skin's ancestors came from hot countries; nothing else is different." From then on, my son would come home from school and say, "Mom, I have a new friend, and his ancestors came from a hot country."

## CHILDREN ARE ALWAYS WATCHING

I remember being six years old and seeing the most authentic, raw fear in a woman. In South Africa, you were looked down on if you could afford to employ other people, but you did not; doing so was seen as helping your community. One day, an African woman named Ellen came to my parents' door and said she had no job, no husband (he had passed away), and children to feed. My parents hired her to help in the house. However, she was not considered legal because she was registered to work in another state. If you hired a person from another state, you were heavily fined by the government (this was part of keeping each tribe separate), and if you were found working in another state, you were arrested and put in jail. Ellen was desperate enough to venture out of her state for work and put herself and her children at incredible risk. My mom and dad could sense Ellen's desperation to find work and decided to risk the possible fine and reprimand to help her family by giving her a job. Ellen was risking so much more.

One day, my mother got a call from a neighbor saying the police, who randomly came to check workers' papers, were coming door to door, and our house was next. My mother grabbed Ellen, ran to my bedroom, and hid her in the wardrobe. With deliberation and focus in her eyes and voice, my mom told Ellen to stay there and keep quiet! I watched my mother magically transform herself into the coolest, calmest person, and walk toward the window to wait for the police to come up the driveway. She realized I was also a part of this problem and turned to me. Holding my shoulders, with absolute clarity, she told me I was not to open my mouth, and I had to keep completely quiet no matter what she said.

The police came to our house and knocked on the door. There were two, large, mustached white men in khaki uniforms, with pistols and batons on their hips; they were terrifying. They firmly asked my mom if she had a domestic worker. She calmly said no, that she did all her own cleaning. They glanced down at me, standing there with my doll in my arms, then tried to look past us into the house. I could tell they were looking for something. I do not know how, but I showed no expression, even though my heart was beating so fast. I did not understand why the police would want the wonderful woman hiding in my wardrobe with my toys.

My mother wished them well and closed the door. She stood there for a few moments, watching them walk down the driveway, get into their police van, and drive away. Then she called the next neighbor to warn them. We both went to my room to tell Ellen they were gone. The vision of Ellen when she opened the door was something I had never seen before, nor since. Ellen was so terrified she could not even stand up. She had tears running down her face and her lips were quivering as my mom helped her up, and then Ellen let out the hardest cry I have ever heard. My mom cried with her, acknowledging the possibility of what could have happened to her. The difference was, if my mom were caught, she would get reprimanded and fined. If Ellen were caught, she would have been thrown in jail and possibly beaten. After that day, I never saw Ellen again; she never came back to work.

Children see everything parents do, right or wrong, and they understand the difference. On that day, I saw my mother do the right thing and take the hard *right* over the easy *wrong*. I might not have fully understood everything at six years old, but I realized my parents were helping someone. They saw a person first. They saw a family in need of help, and no matter the consequences, they would do what they could to help.

What we say and do in our daily life, through our actions, conversations, and habits, has an incredible influence over children. Children watch everything we do as parents and hear everything we say; even if they do not fully understand it in the moment, they still hear. Knowing this, I always ask myself: Are we setting the right example for our kids? Are we speaking in ways that express the values we want our children to have? Are we behaving in a manner that demonstrates right over wrong? Are we doing this daily? Some days, yes, some days, no, but even after all the years that have passed since Ellen left, I still hold this lesson close to my heart.

I often have to take a moment to catch myself when I know I am not doing the right thing. And I hate to say this, but I get lazy—it happens more than I would like to admit. I sometimes yell at the person who cuts me off on the highway. I occasionally let out a curse word (okay, quite often). Regardless of the reason, whether right or wrong, my daily actions influence my kids' development.

It is daunting to remind ourselves of this influence, but it is critical to our children's growth. Every single day, for an average of eighteen years, we impress on our children our version of right and wrong. Whether we like it or not, how our children turn out as adults starts with what we do and what we say every single day.

### *HOWZIT, SAWUBONA, DUMELA, THOBELA, HOE GAAN DIT, MOLO, UJANI?*

(South African greetings in seven languages.)

Think about the last time someone greeted you with absolute

warmth, the last time someone's face showed you how happy they were to see you, the last time you shook someone's hand and felt all their attention, the last time you received a thank you that was so strong in sentiment that the words were irrelevant—that is how it feels to be greeted in South Africa every day.

I have brought this warm South African greeting into my family and my daily life because I want my kids to look into someone's eyes and greet them with full and warm attention. In South Africa, you always ask how someone is, then give a handshake (usually a three-part handshake). Some even put their left hand on the side of the other person's hand or their left hand on their elbow. South Africans do this to signify that all their attention is on the person they are greeting. The greeting then flows into asking about each other's health, no rush, no distractions. That is how I want to be greeted and how I want my children to make others feel. There is something special about being seen intently and teaching our kids to see others intently and not just skim past them.

## MARIA'S GREETING

After Ellen left, my parents hired a full-time domestic worker. Maria was a part of my life for nearly twenty years. She was a tiny, but very proud Zulu woman. Maria had a few teeth missing and always wore her hair exactly the same, with African braids perfectly done. I do not remember much of growing up before her.

I felt like Maria was one of the most special people in my life. She had two sons and called me her only daughter. She was always there, always listening, and always helping me in some way. The best part of my relationship with Maria was that when I came home from school mad at someone who had wronged my teenage self, she would get upset with that person with me and then follow up with some wisdom to help me let it go. I loved her so much. At my wedding, she sat at the head table with my parents as one of my most treasured people. She holds a much bigger story that does not fit in this book, but I want to share how she greeted me each morning.

Before school, I would come into the kitchen dressed in my school uniform. Maria would stop whatever she was doing, look me straight in the eyes with a huge smile on her face, do a little hip wiggle, and sing, with the highest-pitched, happiest melody, "Hello, my angel!" Hearing her voice in my head still brings me to tears because this greeting was heart-lifting each and every day. Maria taught me how it feels for someone to be truly happy to see you. I felt loved and wanted by her every day.

To honor Maria and the lesson she taught me, I give the same kind of greeting to my kids. Every morning, I light up when I see them waking up, tell them I missed them, and show on my face how happy I am they are in my life. I want them to know every day they are loved and wanted.

This type of profoundly personal greeting is similar to the Maori greeting in New Zealand. It is an incredible feeling. My family went to a Maori village on the South Island and were greeted in a way that felt like time stopped, just like I felt every morning with Maria. The chief we met came up to us, and with no rush, put his forehead against mine and held it there until we had connected, "breathing the same breath," as they explain it. The greeting with our heads pushed together ends when it ends and is held until it is done. In that moment, you get to feel the other person truly, and then you are connected. I was in awe of how good it felt to be greeted this way. It is different from South African greetings, but the feeling you have when you are seen and connect with another is incredibly similar.

In Fiji, you are greeted with a loud "*Bula!*"—a blessing of love, life, and good health. In Hawaii, you are greeted with "*Aloha*," meaning kindness, unity, pleasantness, humility, and patience.

Forevermore, I will honor Maria, the Maoris, the Fijians, the Hawaiians, and every culture that greets with love and compassion by greeting my children with love and affection each and every day. Then, once they are reminded how much they are loved, we can deal with real life and the probability that their hair needs washing before we go out and their socks don't match.

## BABY GOT BACK

*"The pram is the ultimate in pushing the baby away from you. The baby on the back is actually following the mother in warmth and comfort. The baby feels safer, and safer people are happier people."*

— *Frank Njenga, child psychiatrist, Nairobi, Kenya*

When I was thirty-one, I went back to South Africa with my daughter, who was just under three months. My husband, a US Army officer, deployed to Afghanistan for a year, so I decided to go back home to further my education while he was away. Everything was planned perfectly. My parents were there to help me with my daughter when I was at school. I was able to focus on my studies, my brand-new baby, and try not to think about my husband being in a war zone. What wasn't planned for was my mother breaking her arm three weeks after I arrived and not being able to pick up my nine-week-old baby. We had to look for help, and we found a wonderful, willing woman, Lindiwe, who looked after both my mom and daughter on the days I was at the university. Lindiwe had a two-year-old at the time and was a beautiful mama. She and I became genuinely close. (She was looking after my most precious person, so how could we not?) We would get into some great discussions about the differences in how people live and parent. She always wanted to hear about America and how Americans parent. But one particular conversation stopped me in my tracks, and I will never forget it.

We took the kids out for lunch. In South Africa, there are incredible restaurants for both parents and children, places where you can go and let your child run free on tricycle tracks, in play houses, on playgrounds, and experience so much imaginative play. The restaurants hire people to watch the kids in case the parent turns away and misses a fall. There are arcade games, make your own pizza areas, and little picnic tables for the children to eat at.

Once Lindiwe and I arrived in the parking lot, I took my pram (stroller) out of the car while she put her two-year-old on her back with a colorful piece of long fabric, as nearly every South African mother does. She bluntly said, "Why do you white women put your babies in prams?"

I was stunned; why wouldn't we? I could tell she wanted to share her thoughts. "I just don't understand," she continued, "why you would push your child into the street first." Her words hit me like a ton of bricks. We did do that. We pushed our most precious babies into the street first, ahead of ourselves! She continued, "If a car comes out of nowhere, I can protect my child by using my body; you can't do anything."

I could not answer her; here I was so proud of my brand-new pram, and now I was looking at it so differently. From her African cultural perspective, she felt it was easier to protect a baby on her body than to be separate from a child in a pram. Statistically, I don't know which one is safer, but I did get exactly where she was coming from; ultimately, all parents want to protect their babies. After our lunch, I asked Lindiwe to take me to a shop so I could buy a long piece of African fabric, and she could teach me how to carry my baby on my back. Months later, after learning to love my baby on my back, I upgraded from African fabric to a more "Western" Ergobaby carrier. But Lindiwe's perception of parenting changed my life. I was amazed at how an open, honest discussion between parents from two different worlds could change your parenting life for the better.

I did continue to use my pram on occasion, but it usually carried my shopping. Carrying my kids on my back was, by far, my favorite way to move around.

## SLEEP *MUTI*

*Muti* is South-African traditional medicine. Sleep *muti* is not medicine at all, but my dad's brilliant idea to get my brother Martin and me to sleep when we were struggling to fall asleep. It works like a charm! The only rule with sleep *muti* is you have to believe in it 100 percent. You cannot falter or doubt it in any way, or it will not work. Here is how to use it:

If my kids cannot fall asleep, I offer them sleep *muti*, or sometimes they ask for it on their own. I get a glass, fill it a quarter full of milk, and then warm it in the microwave—not hot, just warm. Then I add a teaspoon of honey and a dash of cinnamon. I bring the sleep *muti* to them in bed and sit them up. I offer to hold them because the *muti* will work fast, and they might not get through the whole glass. I often have to hold my laughter as I see their eyelids droop while they hold the glass and look at me in amazement at how well the *muti* is working. I take the glass from them, help them down on the pillow, and they fall asleep right away. It is incredible how powerful a child's imagination is. Sleep *muti* just uses that imagination for the parent and child's benefit.

You, of course, can make your own sleep *muti* any way you want depending on your child's tastes and needs. You can even make it in a special glass only used for sleep *muti*. My kids always ask what is in this magic mixture, and I say every time, "I cannot tell you…it is a parenting secret. You can only find out when you become a parent."

## LESSONS LEARNED

- Children see everything parents do, right or wrong, and they understand the difference (see "Children Are Always Watching" above).

- What we say and do, through our actions, conversations, and habits, has an incredible influence on children.

- How our children turn out as adults starts with what we do and what we say every day.

- There is something special about being seen intently and teaching our kids to see others intently.

- Greet your children with warmth, happiness, and love each morning (see "Maria's Greeting").

- Show your children they are loved and wanted.

- Everyone parents differently, but that does not mean anyone's parenting is wrong (see "Baby Got Back").

# CHAPTER 2

# POSITIVE BRAINWASHING

*"There are two things we should give our children:
one is roots, and the other is wings."*

*— Unknown*

E ighteen years—that is all we really have. Eighteen years to fill our children with goodness and give them most of what they need to grow into prosperous adults. After eighteen years, a lot of what our children will learn will come from experiences outside the home. Our time with them and ability to influence them will dwindle and our role will most likely change from parent to mentor, which is a completely different kind of parenting. So, while we have our children and can still brainwash influence them, let's do it positively.

## THOMAS EDISON'S MOTHER

While writing *Think and Grow Rich*, Napoleon Hill documented and interviewed the most successful people of his time. Published in 1937, the book shares successful people's success formulas; nearly a century later, it continues to motivate people all over the world. Hill found that success is not determined by age, race, gender, education, finances, or any perceived disadvantage; he concluded that success is all about how you think.

The book, and years later the movie *Think and Grow Rich: The Legacy*, starts with a compelling story about Thomas Edison and shows the importance of a parent in building a child. The story goes something like this:

In 1854, seven-year-old Thomas Edison sat in his home on a couch holding a letter with a red wax seal on the back. The letter was addressed to his mother. She came into the room and was startled to find Thomas was not at school. When she joined him on the couch, he gave his mom the letter; she broke the seal and read it silently. Then she looked at Edison and proceeded to read it out loud to him: "Your son is a genius. This school is too small for him and does not have enough trained teachers to teach him. Please teach him yourself." She smiled at him and gave him a proud hug.

She began teaching young Thomas and poured her love and belief into him daily over many years.

The story then jumps to Thomas Edison's study many years later. Edison is sitting in his office going through paperwork and finds the letter with the red wax seal on the back. He opens it and reads, "Mrs. Edison, your son is mentally slow and unable to think clearly. We will not let him come to school anymore." It was signed by the school principal.

Napoleon Hill found that every life has many potentials. The difference between a traditional life and an extraordinary life hinges on the way people think. In Thomas Edison's case, it shows we are taught to believe. Thank goodness Mrs. Edison did not let young Thomas believe what the principal had come to feel; otherwise, the world could have been very different.

Unfortunately, Hill decided to embellish the truth a little to make the story better. There never was a letter. Instead, Mrs. Edison went down to the school to speak to the principal. She chose only to tell Edison positive things after her meeting. The main point is that Edison's mother played an influential role in his becoming one of the greatest inventors of all time. This story, and the parenting displayed by Mrs. Edison, can teach us all a few lessons. First, the power we hold in certain moments of our parenting journey can be what feeds our children for the remainder of their lives. Those rare moments can be life defining if we, as parents, do and say the right things. That moment when Mrs. Edison decided to tell her son what she felt instead of accepting the principal's opinion is usually rare in a child and parent's life. But when such moments happen, we must know whether we are speaking out of frustration and anger toward the principal or love and foresight for the child.

More important than those huge moments are the small, everyday moments. What you tell your children every day, they may eventually become. So, the big question here is: What are we telling our children every day that is getting stuck in their heads and shaping their mindsets? Are they hearing positive or negative thoughts? Are they development ideas that create growth or constraining ideas that limit? What we say to our children is incredibly important and shapes their future. So, those precious eighteen years when our children live with us can truly be the most influential time in their lives. It is scary, I know, but it is true.

## HOW TO GROW BAMBOO

In Australia, I had coffee with a wonderful single mom named Lisa. She and her ex-husband split when her daughter was two. We talked when her daughter was thirteen, and Lisa told me their story through the years. Lisa does not have a lot of family support, and the dad is not in the picture anymore. But she is probably one of the most positive and upbeat people I have met, despite all she had to complain about. To top it all off, her daughter is also on the autism spectrum. I asked Lisa how she manages to stay consistent as a mom with no help. (Single mothers are a different species of human, of that I am sure.) Lisa spoke of how all she wanted to do was grow a strong, well-rooted child. The story she shared was a beautiful analogy of what it takes to "grow" a strong child.

Lisa began with a Chinese story about growing bamboo:

> A person was having problems. They struggled with feelings of inadequacy as they were not growing and becoming whom they wanted to become. They had become complacent, wanting to give up and not try so hard anymore.

> This person's mentor asked, "Do you know how long it takes a giant bamboo plant to grow to the size of a building? Let me tell you. During the first year, the tiny plant is looked after by watering and fertilizing it. But nothing happens. The small bamboo plant is then looked after by a farmer with constant water and fertilizing it for another year, and another, and another, but nothing happens…only in the fifth year of consistency and continual pouring of care into it does it shoot up to the sky. In six weeks, the bamboo grows ninety feet.

> "So how long does the bamboo take to grow?" asked the mentor.

> "Six weeks," said the mentee.

> "That is your mistake," the mentor replied. "It takes five years. If the farmer did not water or feed the plant at any point during the five years, it would have shriveled up and died."

> The mentor continued to explain, "Under the ground, the roots were developing to support the bamboo so it would be ready for the sudden growth. Growth takes time, and every drop of care makes a difference. You may not see the growth immediately, but growth is still happening beneath the surface."

The lesson here is every drop of effort you put into your child helps grow their roots and make them stronger. You may not even see the results for months or years, but one day, your child will go out into the world with strong roots and do what they were put on this planet to do. Consistency and care over time is needed to develop a strong child.

## THE *WEE BAIRN'S* OWN STORIES

My family traveled to Edinburgh, Scotland, when my kids were *wee bairns* (little children). The kids do not remember much about Edinburgh, but I think it must be one of my favorite cities. I have been there four times, but only once with children, and each time I go, I make sure I stay in a bed and breakfast (B&B). Why? Because you get to speak to locals and see how they live. My favorite part of traveling is the people you get to meet…and their stories!

On this particular trip, we went with my sister-in-law Dawnele and her two daughters. The train from Birmingham, England, to Edinburgh station took seven hours. On arrival, we checked into a modest B&B. It was home to a lovely Scottish woman whose husband had passed and whose children had grown. Every morning, we went downstairs for breakfast and the "lady of the house" would make us a home-cooked breakfast of eggs, bacon, link sausages, baked beans, and black pudding (dried pig's blood sausage, one of the oldest forms of sausage). The black pudding was usually the only thing we left on our plates. Except for my husband. He eats anything!

One morning, I stayed downstairs to have some more coffee while everyone else popped upstairs to finish getting ready for the day out in the beautiful city. Our host sat at the table with me, sharing a cup of coffee and a chat. We got to talking about children since between my sister-in-law and myself, we had three children under seven and one teen. The woman reminisced about her days as a mom of *wee bairns*. In her strong, melodious Scottish accent, she spoke about how she loved to see children in her home. This home was where she had raised her children from birth. They were in their twenties and thirties now and were starting to get married or think about starting families of their own. Of course, I asked her questions about how she raised her children.

By our second cup of coffee, she revealed something I just loved, hooked myself into, and implemented right away. Even to this day, my children still ask me to do this. I am grateful to our host, although, unfortunately, I can't remember her name. I might have to travel back one day so I can give her the credit she deserves for sharing her incredible nugget of loveliness with our family.

This wise Scottish mom said that each one of us has a special entrance in the world. Everyone's story is a fresh start, and our delivery into the world has so much emotion involved that is not always shared. Most of us hold the day our child is born as a momentous day we will never forget. My new Scottish coffee buddy said that instead of always telling her children fairytales about faraway lands, kings, queens, forgotten slippers, and magic spells, she told them the greatest love story of all: their birth stories.

She told them over and over again, reliving every moment that brought the little bundle into her arms, then expanded the story to what happened next. She shared all the emotions, who was there, what they did and said. She included grandparents, siblings, uncles, aunties, friends, and doctors. She made some parts funny and some parts raw, but mostly, she said, "If you know where you come from, you will always have a place to start."

So, I started telling my kids their birth stories, and I did so often. It was our number one bedtime story. As they grew and matured, their stories grew and matured too.

How did they get here? What was their birth or process of adoption like? Telling children how you came together is a secure bonding experience. Children want us to share our experiences with them. They want to know exactly how much they were wanted and are wanted now—what you craved or how much sleep they needed. How did they kick you? How did it feel to see them for the first time? What did their daddy do when he found out their sexes? All these stories make them feel a part of something bigger, a family unit. Make the stories funny; be entertaining so your children will laugh—that way, the stories take on feelings of joy, laughter, warmth, and belonging.

My daughter's delivery actually fractured my coccyx, and I remind her of this in jest regularly. If I ask her to do something for me, and she does not want to, I remind her whose back she broke. It works every time. (I often get the last piece of chocolate in the box with this tactic.) She asks when I will let this story go, and I say "never!" It is part of her story, and when I am long gone, she will remember all about that monumental day and the events around it, even if she would never remember it herself.

The more about your birth story you know, the more you feel a part of the family. You know and understand your very beginnings on this planet and can see more easily how far you have come already. This can be profound for a three- or four-year-old or a pleasant reminder to a rebellious teenager. To see where they started and compare it to where they are today makes them feel like part of a family—right from day one.

## HELPING YOUR FUTURE SELF

In 2017, I met Sharron, the coolest Harvard-trained doctor and acupuncturist. We met in an aerial yoga class swinging from the rafters, literally. (Aerial yoga is where you hang in a big hammock suspended by chains from the ceiling—super fun.) I immediately liked Sharron because she was undeniably having the best time swinging around and was not afraid to show it. I knew right then that I wanted her in my life; who wouldn't want a doctor-acupuncturist who likes aerial yoga? Sharron and I became friends and would meet up weekly so she could stick needles in me as we chatted. Her children were older than mine, and she always had great stories about their teenage years. One day in her beautiful home office, overlooking a lake and rose garden, Sharron told me about how she always said to her children, "How are you helping your future self?"

At first, I was like, "Your future who?" But after a few more stories and a few more needles, I finally got it. Your future self could be your future self of tomorrow morning, next week, next year, or the next ten years. This idea struck a chord with me, so again, I immediately began to implement it in our family. The concept is not difficult—think and plan for your future, whether that is laying out school clothes for the next morning so your sixteen-year-old is not changing outfits five times before school or studying for a test that will be an important part of your final grade.

Tying this concept to the "self" is where this statement can hit home for children. When you say, "Help future (insert name) by…." or ask the question, "Is this (insert negative action) helping future (insert name)?" it makes it personal to the child, and immediately, more important to them. When a child can realize that, over time, of course, doing things to help themselves in the future, near or far, is actually a really good thing, everyone wins—both you as a parent and your child's future self.

I loved Sharron's idea and used it often. It took a few times for my children to understand the concept, but they ultimately did. Just last week, my daughter said, "Mom, I just need to finish this so I can help my future self." She was referring to the next morning when she knew she would be scrambling to get out the door. It was a small win, but a win nonetheless.

## LESSONS LEARNED

- We have eighteen years to influence our children.

- Our children may become what we tell them (see "Thomas Edison's Mother").

- The power we hold in certain moments of our parenting journey can be what feeds our children for the remainder of their lives.

- Consistency and care over time is needed to develop a strong child…just like bamboo.

- If you know where you come from, you will always have a place to start.

- Teach your children how to help their future selves.

# CHAPTER 3

# PARENTING WISDOM FROM THE UNITED KINGDOM

*"I came to parenting the way most of us do—knowing nothing and trying to learn everything."*

— *Mayim Bialik, actress and neuroscientist*

### FINDING A HOUSE…AGAIN

If there is one thing I have truly enjoyed about the military moving our family all over the world and all the change that comes with it, it is finding wonderful new people who have experiences and talents I couldn't even imagine. Then they end up changing my life in ways I never could have expected. Some people change it in the smallest ways. Some in more significant ways. Sometimes change comes by just watching how a different culture raises its children, and sometimes change comes by meeting parents who are happy to share their parenting experiences.

When I find a freakishly good mom or dad, I call them a "parenting guru." You know the ones I'm talking about. The most amazing mom guru I have ever met started as my landlord, then became my friend, and later one of my most valued life teachers. I met her when my family and I moved from Washington State in the United States to Gloucestershire in the United Kingdom.

Whenever our family moves, we have the luxury of deciding how we want our experience at that next destination to be. We sit down together and discuss how we want those twenty-four months to be—how will we live, what kinds of schools will the kids attend, where do we want to travel, etc. With the UK planning session, I decided I wanted the quintessential Cotswold England experience. In my mind, this meant we would try to find a home in a small village, with narrow, winding roads, a butcher, a baker, and a church that was at least 500 years old (anything younger in England simply would not do). So, we decided on country living, which meant dealing with long commutes to schools.

The experience I envisioned proved harder than we anticipated. Everywhere we looked, something was wrong—the majority of the homes were too small for our large American furniture. Some homes were on a main road; some did not have a garden for the kids to play in; it was always something.

During one of our visits to yet another house that wasn't right for us, a real estate agent overheard Deric and me talking. He asked us to hold on a moment while he went outside to make a call. I overheard him saying, "I think these are the ones you have been looking for." He came back inside and said he had a house available for us to go see the next day, but we'd have to be interviewed by the landlord. What?

The next morning, we gathered up the kids, climbed into a very small rental car, and drove to the address we were given for the viewing and interview. We were dressed in our Sunday best, and brought the children, who were three and five at the time.

For two miles, we drove down winding, extremely narrow lanes with lush green hedges on both sides that grew much higher than our car until we hit a sand driveway. As we drove down the driveway, we crossed a small bridge that passed over a narrow moat with ducks in it. There, tucked away on a large property, was a manor house covered with ivy and a circular driveway. Surrounding the manor was a series of small barns that had been converted into beautiful small homes. In the middle of all the small barns was a larger, rectangular barn with the most beautiful gardens around it, an orchard, six raised vegetable patches, and a rose garden. It was truly the most unusual, amazing house-barn ever!

There, in the driveway, stood a woman in her late fifties or early sixties, tall, secure, and dignified. She was wearing a floral dress, as you would expect all quintessential English women to wear, and I liked her immediately.

Her name was Debbie. She showed us around the house and asked us a dozen or more questions, while watching our every move. After a while, I noticed she was paying more attention to the kids than to Deric and me. She watched them wander around the house and garden. I could tell she loved to see kids in the house.

This property was actually a working dairy farm. Everywhere you looked outside the home, which was an upside-down house (kitchen and living area upstairs, bedrooms downstairs) just to make it more interesting, you could see dozens and dozens of black and white cows. Three other couples lived on the property in other house-barns, but none had children. Since Debbie had raised her children on the farm years earlier, before she converted all the barns into houses, she felt the farm needed the sound of children playing again. Thus, all the questions during the interview and her continuously watching the children. I knew then that Debbie was someone special.

We hadn't talked about rent. We looked at this beautiful home, knowing our budget would never cover such a wonderful experience. Later that day, the agent called us and said we got the house! We felt a bit awkward because we were sure we could not cover the rent. Our agent asked, "What is your budget?" Telling him honestly and then holding our breath, he said, "Yes, that will do." Surprised does not even come close to describing our reaction. In the end, Debbie wanted us—a family on the farm, and we were lucky enough to be in the right place at the right time.

Over the following weeks and months, Debbie and I started a beautiful friendship. She was a magistrate (district judge) and also helped her husband Charles work the dairy farm. Daily, she would walk past The Granary as she took a lunch basket down to the lower cow pastures and barns to eat with her husband. (In England, many homes have names instead of numbers. Ours was "The Granary.")

Debbie invited us for a Sunday roast (dinner) occasionally. By watching her interact with her family, I learned what an amazing mother she was. She became a woman I secretly looked up to and admired dearly. I doubt she ever knew. I wish she did. I used to tell my husband she was the parent I want to be when I grow up.

Her son was twenty-three and would often come to Sunday dinner (an indicator of great parenting all by itself). Debbie and her husband had such an incredible, close relationship with their son. I realized that was what I wanted with my son one day. Debbie and her son were not just mother and son, but friends with respect and admiration for each other. She never had an air of, "I'm your mother...now listen to me." It was so lovely to experience firsthand such a loving parent-child relationship and see what it looked like when the child was an adult. *But how do I get there from here?* I thought to myself. To ensure I would not miss an opportunity to learn from a mom guru, I invited Debbie over for tea (that's what you do in England) and asked her point blank what she did to get a relationship like that with her adult children.

Debbie gave me some of the best advice I have ever received, and I have shared it liberally with anyone who would listen. It is so simple, so easy, and makes so much sense that I just can't believe it is not posted everywhere for all parents to see from the day they find out they are having a baby.

As a magistrate, Debbie said she used to come home from work and tell stories about her day, all the people she encountered, and all the pretty difficult situations. For example, if Debbie was having the drug discussion with her children, she would not stand over them and say, "You should never do drugs!" Instead, she would say something like, "I have to tell you a story about a teenager who came into court today. He sold drugs at school…." She would tell them a story instead of giving them a lecture. Sometimes she would start the stories with, "I shouldn't tell you this, but…" to pique the children's interest, and then, having all of their attention, share a story that included the lesson she wanted to get across. Debbie never barked at her kids; she told them stories to teach lessons. Her children saw her as a storyteller, a parent who did not go into lecture mode. Debbie explained that, as her children grew up, they came to her with every problem and concern imaginable because they knew she would not lecture them or yell at them. Debbie even said her kids' friends would come to her with problems before they would go to their own parents. Debbie simply spoke to her children like people. No lectures, no judgments, and always with a story to deliver a lesson.

Our children are going to be adults longer than they'll be our infants, toddlers, pre-teens, and teenagers combined. Debbie showed me that your relationship with your future adult child is just as important as teaching them to share and eat with a knife and fork. What future relationships are you setting up with your children? How are you helping your future self as a parent and your children as adults? So, I started doing as Debbie did…telling my children stories instead of giving them lectures.

To tell stories effectively, draw on stories from when you were at school, when you were a kid, or even from outside sources—news, friends, anywhere. Become a story collector and a storyteller. It works! Children listen because our ancestors were storytellers. Passing stories down generation after generation is quintessentially human. As a species, we've been telling stories since we started talking. Tap into this genetic parenting gift, and use it to your and your children's advantage.

I will never forget the lessons Debbie taught me during our experience in England. She was an exceptional woman and parent, and I am so glad she shared her story with me over afternoon tea. She was the original inspiration behind my wanting to share stories and lessons, and ultimately, how I structured this book: with parenting lessons taught through stories from around the world.

Take a moment to remember the people who have taught you lessons. Who were these people, and what did they teach you? Are you following their examples? Below, list some of these people and briefly describe what they taught you.

_____

_____

_____

_____

_____

_____

_____

_____

_____

_____

_____

_____

## A 100ᵗʰ BIRTHDAY PARTY

In 2014, my great-aunt Margaret (and she is a *great* aunt) turned 100—as I write, she is now 105. She still lives on her own and plans her own birthday party every year. She is the oldest English Girl Guide (Girl Scout in America) in the world and was given a medal at Buckingham Palace for all she has done for the Girl Guide world. (See…I said she was a *great* aunt!)

At her home in the small English town of Chorley on her 100ᵗʰ birthday, Aunty Margaret sat in her chair counting birthday cards before a church service in her honor. (This church, by the way, was the same church where she had been baptized 100 years ago.) She was secretly hoping to get 100 birthday cards, and she exceeded that number very quickly. She was so proud that she displayed the cards around the house wherever she could find space. And because her apartment was so small and quaint, she even had to use the floorboards to display all her birthday cards.

Aunty Margaret had always given me great advice, some that had reshaped my life. One particular time she really helped me. When I met Deric, I was living and working in London, and he was a young Army officer stationed in Germany. Only three short months after we met, he was going to be deployed to Iraq for a twelve-month combat tour. I was so torn about what to do…wait for him or let him go. I went to Aunty Margaret and told her my situation. Her advice was perfect, and I am still grateful for it today.

Aunty Margaret told me about how she had been in a similar situation during World War II. Only, she had waited for her husband's return for six years, only saw him a few weekends a year, and rarely received letters. Oh, yeah…and there were no phone calls or email back then. Her story shocked me to the core and immediately opened my eyes to how impatient I had become. After that conversation, I called Deric and told him, "Go. I will be here when you come home."

After watching my aunty count her birthday cards, I asked her a question I had wanted to ask her for years: "What is the secret to a long, happy, healthy life?"

She looked at me, surprised, and with a strong British accent, said: "Have a tot of whiskey a day to kill the germs, and mind your own business."

Mind your own business. When these words came out of her mouth, it was like a weight lifted off my shoulders. Then and there, I made an agreement with myself to stay out of other people's business. This especially applies to parenting. Try it. It is so much easier to remove yourself from the natural wonder of keeping up with the neighbors or comparing children's performances. Little Skyler started walking at nine months. Little Finley has already started chewing solid food. Young Reilly got straight As. Young Ridley is playing for the club soccer team. Super-smart Pat just got accepted to the University of Virginia. Bailey just got a promotion. My dog can sit, stay, bark on command, and use a flush toilet.

Who cares! Stop comparing kids and lives. Mind your own business, and do your own best. No more comparisons. No more guilt. No more competition. Just mind your own business; focus on your own family. Honestly, since hearing this, when I feel myself getting sucked into these silly, insignificant situations, I remember these words and think…*mind your own business….*

Don't forget that shot of whiskey a day to kill the germs!

**DID I EVER TELL YOU ABOUT…?**

If you come to my house for breakfast, nine times out of ten, you will be served oatmeal. This is our family's signature before-school breakfast. Not just because it is a healthy meal to start the day, but because oatmeal has a history in my family.

My grandfather, Nampa Tom, was born in 1907, in Chorley, England, the same town as his sister-in-law, Aunty Margaret, and was a young boy during World War I. During the years between 1914 and 1918, he was given oatmeal for breakfast every single day by my great-grandmother. With food rations in those hard days, I am not sure how any mother ever fed her children; as my mom says, "Those mothers are also heroes."

One morning during those hard times, little Tom's mom gave him his daily warm oatmeal for breakfast, and for some reason, he declined it. Slightly surprised, but still composed, she did not fight his refusal. She simply put it on the shelf (no refrigerator...shelf). Lunchtime came, and young Tom went to have his lunch, so she took his oats off the shelf and put them in front of him. He defiantly declined, trying to get bread and butter like his siblings were having, but she just smiled and put it back on the shelf. By dinner, you guessed it, the very cold and now somewhat stale oatmeal was taken off the shelf again and placed in front of young Tom. You can just imagine what the oatmeal must have looked and felt like by then, and guess what, Tom declined it again.

After a full day of not eating anything, this stubborn little boy was incredibly hungry. The next morning, after Tom woke with a hungry, empty tummy, he sat down for breakfast, and yep, the same cold, stale bowl of oatmeal was taken off the shelf and placed in front of him. He ate it. Times were hard, but my great-grandmother was even harder.

When our morning oatmeal goes on the table, I always say, "Did I ever tell you about my Nampa who did not eat his oatmeal?" "Yes!" my kids yell.

One small lesson here is simple. Hungry kids will eat anything, and most of the time, they will like the food you give them because they are so hungry. (That's a win-win.) Now, I'm not advocating starving your kids for a day like my great-grandma. What I am saying is hungry kids eat the food you put in front of them. Without chips, cookies, and whatever snacks between meals, children get hungry.

Then, just like Tom, hungry children will magically eat all their meal, including vegetables, meats, and cold oatmeal.

But the most important lesson from this story is not to get kids to eat their oatmeal or vegetables. It is to show children a different time, a time far removed, and how fortunate they are to get breakfast, lunch, and dinner so quickly every day. The lesson is knowing history and how things have changed. Knowing how war affected families, and how, by keeping family stories alive, their great-great-grandmother can still teach a lesson to her great-great-grandchildren. I know my children will tell their kids this story if they ever serve them oatmeal. So, our family history will continue through a simple bowl of oatmeal.

What are some family stories you want to pass on through your children? Is there a lesson you can tie to these stories? I'm sure there is. Take time now to think about it and record your thoughts below.

Family stories and lessons you would like to pass on:

---------------------------------------------------

---------------------------------------------------

---------------------------------------------------

---------------------------------------------------

---------------------------------------------------

---------------------------------------------------

---------------------------------------------------

---------------------------------------------------

---------------------------------------------------

## LESSONS LEARNED

- Tell your children a story to make a point instead of giving them a lecture.

- Our children are going to be our adult children longer than they will be our babies—secure a relationship now.

- Mind your own business—don't be concerned what other families are doing.

- Tell stories about and from previous generations.

- Kids eat anything when they are hungry.

# CHAPTER 4

# REMEMBERING YOUR IMAGINATION

*"Those who don't believe in magic will never find it."*

— *Roald Dahl*

D
o you remember being a kid? It might have been a while since you really took some time to think about it, but we all should. Start now. Do you remember the games you played? The way cuddly toys made you feel? What you thought about in bed before you fell asleep? How it felt to play a board game? The feelings, smells, and tastes of the dream-like life? Everything was different as a child. Unfortunately, as we grow older, we usually forget this, but it is a big part of how we, as parents, can relate to and find the fun in parenting. Remembering will also help us understand where our children are in their precious lives.

## THE MAGIC WARDROBE

My dad is a kind, creative man who has always said, "When I grow up, I want to be a little boy." I believe it was this mindset that helped him create part of a magical world in my childhood. When we were kids, our father kept something in the garage, something so special and magical that I dreamt about it all week as a child and still remember it in extraordinary detail today. It was the biggest wardrobe

I had ever seen. As a child, it held an indescribable allure for me. And there it was, in my garage, crammed in the corner like a gateway to another universe. But it wasn't just a wardrobe…it was a magic wardrobe!

I was so thankful that our home was the keeper of this magnificent, one-of-a-kind, magic wardrobe. How could I have been so lucky? There was only one magical key for this immovable monstrosity, and for some strange reason, it would only open on Sundays and only if my brother Martin and I had been good for the entire week. Inside the wardrobe were my parents' old toys from the 1940s and 1950s.

Martin and I would stand in front of the wardrobe in awe—it held such power. Sometimes on a weekday, I would just sit and stare at it for ages, seeing if anything would happen if I just watched it. The incredible magic was only activated on Sundays after church. When the day finally arrived each week, my parents, brother, and I would all gather together, the key would be inserted into the key hole, and my dad would turn it slowly. A click would follow, and the door would slowly open.

It must have been an incredibly heavy door. I knew this because of the effort my dad expended to open it. My mother would stand behind him with an expression of excitement on her face, while my brother and I would stand in front of the wardrobe and hold our breath in anticipation of what was to come next.

There, in this dusty garage each week, my heart would stop, my breathing would slow, and my mind would explode with imagination overload. The anticipation was just too much. Would it open? Had we been good enough? Did it see me taking Martin's sweets? When the wardrobe did finally open, the relief and excitement was so exhilarating that I literally believed this average Sunday was the greatest day in the history of the world. There was, however, one condition with this magical wardrobe—all of the very special toys had to be returned by sunset or you faced the wrath of an angry magic wardrobe…and I absolutely did not want to deal with that!

That was the story my six-year-old mind believed. In actual fact, the magical wardrobe was an old metal filing cabinet from the 1960s that probably did not even need a key to open. But we would hold our breath each Sunday praying it would open, signifying to our parents that we had been good kids. Most times it would open, but occasionally, it would not, which just made the whole ordeal even more exciting. On the days it didn't open, I am sure my mom and dad found out I had gotten into Martin's sweets!

This is what I mean by remembering how the world looked to you as a child. Anything could happen, and everything was possible. Do you remember?

Before you say, "I don't remember what it's like to be a kid," "I have no imagination," "I live in the real world," "I do not have time," and/ or "I can't relate to kids' games anymore," stop and think about it— because most likely, that is not exactly true. You just don't have the tools, ideas, and inspiration yet. (Notice I said yet. That's where this book comes in.)

## IT'S BARBIE TIME

I will be honest and say there are some kids' activities I cannot stand. If I have to watch anything to do with *The Lego Movie*, I want to cry. My kids love it so much, even their alarm is the theme song—"Everything Is Awesome!" (Cringe. Cringe. Cringe.) There are games my kids don't even ask me to join in on. If parents end up playing games we do not enjoy, we will not have any fun, and the kids will not benefit at all. So, do not do what you do not enjoy. Children will soon learn what to involve you in and what to leave you out of.

When Deric and I got married, we moved from Europe to Fayette-ville, North Carolina. This was a culture shock for sure because it was my first time living in the United States. We bought our first house and settled ourselves into married life. Living across the street from us was an incredible family. They had two children at the time, and I became good friends with the mom, Stephanie. She was the first woman I watched like a hawk to see how she raised her fabulous kids. One day as we were chatting on the street, she looked at her watch and said, "I'm sorry; I have to go. It's Barbie time."

Who says that? And what is Barbie time?

Barbie time was when Stephanie focused only on her youngest; both of them got down on the floor together to play Barbies. This time was joyful for Stephanie because she enjoyed playing Barbies as a child too, and in these moments, she could find that childhood Stephanie and connect with her precious daughter.

After figuring out why Stephanie had Barbie time with her daughter, I decided to become a collector of moms' advice and wisdom every chance I could—to find ways not only to give my kids a great childhood, but also to give myself the best mommy experience, too, because that is just as important.

**FAIRIES CAN BE EVERYWHERE**

I am a talker and have always been, especially as a young girl. As a child, the world looked so inviting and intriguing that I could not help but speak of everything I saw, every minute I was awake. My poor mother used to crave a few moments of silence whenever she could find them. To find some of those precious quiet moments, she used her imagination.

To get to our home in South Africa, we had to pass between two small hills with a long drop on one side of the road. The small hills, or *koppies* as we called them, were filled with trees, bushes, large rock formations, and life. The road passing the *koppies* was quite long, and as we got close, Mom would say, "Shh…look for the fairies." She told me the fairies lived at the bottom, in between the two *koppies*, and I had to be very, very quiet to see them as we drove past. If I made a noise, they would not come out. I looked out the window with such intensity, hoping that *today* was the day I would get to see just one. I would sit quietly, not making a sound, staring intently out the window for minutes as we drove home. Some days, I was convinced I saw a little sparkle, and I would be filled with joy for the rest of the day. And for those precious few minutes, a little girl was quiet for her mom.

Magic can be anywhere…for a child and for a parent! Can you imagine how she felt to see her little girl dreaming of fairies, wonder, and magic? On a regular drive home, she gave me that dream by using a little imagination in a fun game and found a few quiet minutes.

When I go home to South Africa, I drive by those same two koppies and tell my kids the same story. And interestingly enough, they stay quiet, looking for those same fairies. The cycle of magic and fun continues.

If you have been to a Disney resort or heard stories from others who have gone, you have heard parents say they are glad to have kids so they can go to Disney and feel like a child again. Well, I am here to tell you that you do not need a trip to Disney to feel that way. It can be done daily in your own home. Our children, our little, wonderful people, give us the gift of remembering how to be kids all over again.

I am not saying you have to play all day; I think I would rather eat bees, and it is not possible, anyway, with the responsibilities of daily life. But the shortest time spent playing with your children, even just five minutes here or there, can make the biggest difference in your kids and in you; kids have no concept of time like adults do. Time is something we adults learn to obey over a lifetime. It is all about just sprinkling some love and magic over your little ones to help provide some fun detail or excitement to their day, leaving the rest up to them. That's all it takes. Magic!

## TEDDY LOVE

A family counselor introduced me to the concept of respecting your child's relationship with their stuffed toys. This was an idea I had never considered. But this well-respected counselor, who dealt with many issues on childhood trauma and how they could be carried into adulthood, gave me an idea that would forever change how I treated my child's cuddly toys.

She told me about a woman she counseled who had terrible relationships. The woman never trusted that new partners would stick around. After much digging, the counselor and the woman found that at the age of six, the woman's parents had taken away her teddy, believing she was too old for it. What they did not see was that she actually had a relationship with it and mourned its loss for many years.

It got me thinking about my son's love for his special toys and how he believes his love and touch keeps them alive. Devin has names and stories for each one. Until that point, I had never thought he might actually have relationships with them. I came home that day and told Deric what the counselor had shared, and we decided to give more respect to his stuffed animals and how he feels about them.

We no longer throw them across the room when they are on the floor; we refer to them by name, and when he asks us to give them a hug, we do without question.

The idea made me think about the comic strip *Calvin and Hobbes* by

Bill Watterson. It is about the relationship and adventures a six-year-old boy has with his sarcastic stuffed tiger. While everyone else sees Hobbes as an inanimate toy, Calvin sees human qualities and traits in Hobbes—and a friend who shares his lessons and experiences.

Respecting their stuffed friends helps me avoid belittling my children's experiences and enjoy how they see the world, relationships, and imaginative adventures.

## WHO WERE YOU WHEN YOU WERE LITTLE?

Remember the games you loved playing as a kid. Take yourself back to that time. Did you like playdough or coloring? What was your favorite board game? Did you enjoy drawing or making things? Were you crafty? How about woodworking, sewing, baking, or cooking? All these things can be done with your kids, and by doing them, they will have your full attention, and you won't go crazy. Perfect.

So how do you overcome inner objections? Play with some of the ideas on the following pages, and then make them your own. You know that silly six-, eight-, ten-, and twelve-year-old child you use to be? Yes, I know you were once a young, carefree, little human. Where is that person? I guarantee that fun, imaginative, and carefree joker is in there somewhere. Dig deep. Try to remember how it felt to be a kid. I mean, really how it felt. How did grown-ups make you feel? If good, do that; if not good, don't do that. Go through the games you used to play. Remember how a piece of grass could keep you interested for...I have no idea how long because, again, time is irrelevant to a child.

Try to remember how the moments felt when you look back at being a child; don't just see the memories in your mind's eye. Attach to the feeling of each moment, and it will be easier to create or recreate an adventure you might like to share with your kids.

Try it:

1. Close your eyes.

2. Find one good memory from your childhood.

3. Look around like you are still there. See as much detail as you can— the colors, the people, everything you can get out of that moment.

4. Let the feeling come with that memory.

5. Allow yourself to go into the moment entirely.

6. What did you see? How did you feel?

Write it down now while it is still clear in your mind:

_____

_____

_____

_____

_____

What would you do differently to make that moment even better?

_____

_____

_____

_____

_____

If we can remember, we can parent from that angle, and you know what happens next...you start enjoying the process. Guys, it is a blast! And you actually might be surprised what your kids like. You do not have to buy games or toys from Amazon or live on Pinterest to find new, incredible ways to create magic. Just find a moment in your child's day and sprinkle magic into it.

Take some time now to remember being that cute little person you were. Give yourself a few moments to think.

Once you have thought about it, answer the questions below.

Write five games you loved to play as a child (any age).

Examples to draw from: Tag, Hide-and-Seek, Chutes and Ladders (Snakes and Ladders), Catch.

1. _____

2. _____

3. _____

4. _____

5. _____

Write five memories you have playing as a child.

Examples to draw from: Riding a bike, climbing trees, swimming, pool time, reading.

1. _____

2. _____

3. _____

4. _____

5. _____


Write five ways you can bring these memories into your child's life today.

Examples to draw from: hiking, board games, drawing, bedtime stories.

1. _____

2. _____

3. _____

4. _____

5. _____


## LESSONS LEARNED

- Everything can become magic...even an old wardrobe.

- Find games/activities you used to like as a child, and play those games with your children. You will not mind and they will love it.

- Sometimes games can actually give parents a break (see "Fairies Can Be Everywhere").

- Respect your child's imagination; it might be more important than you think (see "Teddy Love").

# CHAPTER 5

# PARENTING LESSONS FROM GERMANY

*"Eltern werden ist nicht schwer, eltern sein dagegen sehr."*
*(It's not hard to become parents, but it is hard to be parents.)*

— *German Saying*

## GRAND TOUR DRIVER'S LICENSES

Our family are massive *Grand Tour* fans. (If you do not know, *Grand Tour* is a car show with three gentlemen who love cars.) I often find my husband, daughter, and son captivated by the show, which sometimes is very naughty and leaves me yelling at my husband for letting them watch it. On one occasion, I got drawn into the conversation one of the characters, James May, was having about Germans. I thought this explained how I first viewed Germany when we lived there.

James May told a story about himself and two friends, one from California and one from Germany. They were talking about losing your driver's license, and the Californian asked, "What would happen if you lost your license and still drove your car?"

"No, you cannot do this," the German said.

"Yeah, I know you are not supposed to, but what if you did?" the Californian asked.

"No! You cannot drive if you have no license," the German said, more deliberately.

"Yeah," repeated the Californian, pressing the question, trying to find the loophole as Americans do, "but, you know, one night you go for a drive and don't have your license...."

"*It is impossible to drive without a license!*" the German responded with full force.

This is how I first viewed Germany. There are rules, and everybody follows them. When everyone follows the rules, it makes life more comfortable, and there is a calmness all over Germany that is truly lovely.

We lived in Germany twice, once before we had kids and once with kids. I was always amazed how people did the right thing, and if you did not, you did not have to worry—there was always someone to tell you where you had gone astray. The first time I took notice of how serious the rules were was the day I found a fine on our recycling trash cans. I had apparently put a piece of rolled-up foil in the plastic container by mistake. The penalty was big enough to make me think about the trash police each time I threw something away in one of our four trash cans.

Regardless, we loved everything about Germany—the food, the fests, the town squares, the bread...oh, the bread! However, I had to give up all my small talk training from the United States because in Germany, most people are not interested in small talk at all. Do not mistake this for being rude (although some easily could), because once you become friends with a German, and you are in their lives, you will see the warmth and genuine care that comes out of this culture.

*FAMILIE IST NICHT EINE WICHTIGE SACHE. SIE IST ALLES.*

(Family is not an important thing. It's everything. — German saying)

If you asked my kids which country they would want to move back to, they would say without hesitation, Germany. Why is this? It is because of how they treat children and also how much they invest in families. There are so many activities for families to enjoy together that, in all our time in Germany, we could not get to everything. Even Oktoberfest in Munich caters to children. During the day, you see families enjoying the tents, rides, and oom-pah bands, but the nights are considered for adults. Even if we took our kids to restaurants on an average weekend night, as a good American family does, it was guaranteed our kids would be the only children in the restaurant.

The pools are probably another reason my kids would move back to Germany. Many are year-round facilities, and they are something you have to see to believe. But the hardest decision of all is deciding which pool to go to first. Do you want indoor or outdoor? Do you want a spa attached? Would you like salt rooms, mud baths, sulphur baths? A swim-up bar to grab cocktails? Slides? Wave pools? Connected hotel with your pool? Would you like to camp out at the pool? Maybe you would like the naked pools or textile-free areas? Whatever you feel like is available, and it is all fun!

Water parks had very few safety monitors or lifeguards. At the entrance of each slide, a list of rules explained who could go on it, how big they should be, etc. Everyone followed the rules, so there was no need to have someone keep order. Why would they need to? There was a sign that clearly explained everything. When everyone follows the rules, you do not have the feeling someone is watching you. But if something goes wrong, you are 100 percent liable, because there was a sign, and you made the decision not to follow the rules. Simple.

The outdoor pools had more than just your typical pools, slides, and diving boards. They had engineering stations in the massive sandpits where children could design waterways. There were zip lines and rope-climbing structures, and no park had plastic "safe areas." They were usually all-metal, most of the time stainless steel, some of it potentially dangerous, and they were awesome.

If your car breaks down on the highway in Germany, you are fined because it is your responsibility to make sure your vehicle is road-worthy. Everyone is responsible for themselves and their own safety. This philosophy, in turn, makes the whole community safe. Likewise, Germans teach their children to be accountable for their safety and to follow the rules. This is where Germany and its culture provided me with so many parenting lessons. Like I said at the beginning of the chapter, it was normal for kids to be out and about during the day, but at night, you did not see them. It was not unusual in smaller villages to see a six-year-old on their own on a bike going to or coming home from school. Children are given freedom and encouraged to be independent.

On the sometimes very intimidating ski slopes in the German Alps, you would see young children around three years old, some still with pacifiers in their mouths, left for the whole day with instructors at a ski school. I was in awe of these little ones, who would be skiing with a pacifier on their own, and not concerned at all. I know this because one year, our kids joined a ski school for a few days when they were four and six. I stood there the whole time in the freezing snow because I was not comfortable leaving them alone with the instructor who spoke just a little English. Some of the Europeans on the slopes thought it amusing I could not leave my kids with strangers for six hours. Still, I got to watch other families and cultures on the ski slopes, and to me, that was the best part.

All the children were taken care of beautifully. There were no tantrums and no whining; they knew their parents were spending the day on the more significant slopes, and they would see them later. I was intrigued and amazed all at the same time.

German stores have play areas set up like little shops for children, with play food, checkouts, and carts, so parents can leave their children in the play area and shop on their own. When you were finished shopping, you would collect your child from the play area (with no one watching them) and make your way to the checkout station. There, the counter person would reach for a special box under the register and happily give each child a small packet of gummy bears. Shopping with kids was actually pleasant for parents and fun for children.

Despite all the goodness just mentioned, Christmas markets must have been my favorite part of living in Germany. Again, there was something for everyone—from puppet shows to princesses (real princesses, too) reading stories to children to *glühwein* (warm, sweet red wine), beer tents, and all kinds of sausages and pastries—more to do than you had time for—for the adults. Cold, fresh, country air with a hint of smoke from the open firepits spread throughout the market. It was a little piece of German heaven.

Child time, family time, adult time—that is how I saw Germans living their lives. Everything closes at 5 p.m. during the workweek. Saturday's close time is 1 p.m., and nothing is open on Sunday. It is family time, none-negotiable. Germany taught me the importance of time. The importance of time with your children and the importance of time without your children.

Time plus entertainment for the whole family is incredibly bonding and can create so many memories. But letting children have time without you can instill independence from a very early age.

German parenting made me see how we can separate our needs as parents and our children's needs into groups so everyone in the family gets what they need. So many times, as parents, we sacrifice our needs or wants for our children (like standing in the snow for six hours of ski lessons). I learned in Germany that when we give our children time to learn how to be with other adults and time to develop their independence, they can become stronger while we get time as adults to be adults.

Then, when kid time and adult time are both done, we can give everyone fun family time in environments that will, hopefully, make memories for a lifetime.

By the end of our stay in Germany, I could let the kids go a bit farther on their own, and it did make me a calmer and more relaxed parent.


## *DEUTSCH SCHULE*

(German Schools)

German schools focus on the comfort of the child as well as their education. Children in elementary school would wear boots to school and then change into slippers they had in cubbies outside their classrooms. I once asked a teacher why the school had the kids wear slippers. She told me it was important for the children to feel comfortable in a place where they spent so much time. Children spend between thirty and thirty-five hours a week at school, and if they are uncomfortable, it will come through in their work, she explained.

Schools also had fruit stations outside the classes. As children move around the halls, they have the option to grab some grapes, orange slices, or cheese and crackers to keep their energy up until lunch. The teacher explained that if they kept feeding growing kids healthy food, they would not be tired or hit those slumps they so often get. This made sense to me.

## KRAMPUSNACHT

(Krampus Night)

Many European nations celebrate the feast of St. Nicholas on December 6 with grand meals and St. Nicholas/Father Christmas/Santa coming through the local village to reward well-behaved children with sweets and gifts. But the evening of December 5, especially in Germany, is very different. Krampus Night or Krampusnacht, is when the wicked, hairy devil Krampus appears on the streets and outside your house. He swats "wicked" children, then stuffs them in his sack, taking them away from their parents and to his lair. German children would burst into tears when they saw him approach and hide behind their parents, screaming with fright as Krampus moved through the village looking for the wicked children. This entire spectacle, and it was a full of spectacle, was the most surprising part of German parenting. How could such a profoundly religious country still keep this pagan tradition where a horned man who was half-goat, half-demon, came through the streets looking to punish children who had misbehaved?

The funniest part of this whole Krampus tradition/spectacle was how well-behaved German children were. And that parents would purposely place their crying children right in front of Krampus each year when he came through the village, reminding them that there were consequences for bad actions. Children would remember that Krampus was going to go through the town each year to capture all the misbehaving kids. Then it was Krampus, not the parents, who was terrifying children into good behavior. It's an interesting parenting technique for sure, and it made me think maybe Krampus was why none of the German children acted out on the ski slopes.

## DEVELOPING INDEPENDENCE

When I went to the local German store for groceries, I always stopped at the attached bakery. I was surprised to see so many young children on bicycles with baskets on the front running out for bread. They would take the money to buy what they needed and go home. This type of childhood independence is rarely seen in the United States. And even as an adult in Germany, I was a little terrified to go up to the baker, butcher, or anyone in service with my broken German language skills. It did get me thinking, though, what if we put our kids in situations where they would have to cope and figure it out? I decided to try an experiment. I gave my then seven-year-old daughter my change purse (you always need change to pay for the toilet in Germany) and had her buy bread in a different language, with foreign currency. I told Kailey what we needed and told her to go.

I stood outside the shop to avoid jumping in to "save the day" and let it happen naturally. Each and every time I did this, Kailey would come out with exactly what I needed, the correct change, a bag of gummy bears, and a big smile.

Then I thought even further. If I put my daughter in uncomfortable situations more often, with people who were not only different from her but whose language she did not speak, how would she later see the big world? Would that help her with fear? Would it help her talk to someone who intimidates her?

Kailey still shows no fear when she has to ask anyone a question or speak to adults. None at all. She would be happy to ask the President of the United States a question or give a speech to her school without hesitation. Implementing this concept with my introvert son Devin has proven to be a bit harder, but I give him no other option. I purposely place him in situations where he is uncomfortable, like a good German parent would, and make him figure it out. As a human being in our increasingly populated and diverse world, children should be able to ask adults questions in any situation and learn to speak to anyone comfortably, no matter how hard it is initially.

## THE BÜRGERMEISTER

(Town master or mayor)

My family was fortunate enough in Germany to become friends with our village mayor and his lovely wife. They were an elderly couple and would invite us to many of the village events as their American guests. Although their English was not excellent, and our German was horrible, they still managed to teach us two valuable lessons.

One was about travel, and it completely changed my view of languages. When discussing our travels around Europe, the mayor's wife reminded me that when you visit a country that does not speak your language, and you don't speak their language, if they choose to speak to you in your language (in this case English), it is a courtesy, not a requirement. She said sometimes she felt English speakers from all over the world thought it was their right to be spoken to in English. It is not. I loved that perspective, and it changed how I traveled and dealt with people. I always try to speak in their language, then ask if they speak mine, and always leave the conversation complimenting their English and thanking them for making it easy on me. It has changed my interactions altogether. How this relates to parenting, I do not know, but it was excellent advice nonetheless.

The second lesson this couple taught us was about setting up expectations for children. Like I said previously, we were always amazed at how well-behaved German children were. They were quiet, too, but only when necessary. Germany is a very quiet country; from restaurants to airports to shops, you never hear screaming kids or anyone shouting.

I asked the mayor's wife, a mother of two, and a grandmother of two, why this was the case. She spoke of how she raised her children always to know her expectations. Wherever the family went, the children would understand the conduct expected in that environment because their mother would clearly explain her expectations to them.

If they were going to church, she would say, "We are going to church now, and you need to sit still and be calm the whole way through the service. After church, you can play outside with all the other children and have a wonderful time." So, before they even arrived at church, the expectation was laid out and understood. In a shop, the children were told to stay quiet, close, and not to ask for anything. If they were going to a pool or a park, they knew they could make as much noise as they wished, because again, the mother would clearly explain her expectations. She continued, "If you allow your kids to act as they wish in any environment, how can they learn to act as adults in a professional workplace?" No one acts as they want to whenever they want. So why would we let our children behave that way? How else will the children learn what is acceptable behavior and what is not?

## PROST!

According to German law (*Jugendschutzgesetz*—protection of young person's act), minors fourteen years of age and older may drink undistilled alcoholic beverages, such as wine and beer, when accompanied by a custodial person. Minors sixteen years of age and older may drink undistilled alcoholic beverages, such as wine and beer, without accompaniment.

Only when we moved to Germany and saw teenagers at beer fests or in restaurants drinking with their parents did I start looking into this law. Our minds were blown coming from the hard and fast rule in the United States of prohibiting anyone under twenty-one from touching alcohol. Seeing teens fourteen and up enjoying a beer or wine with their parents, grandparents, and family, it took a lot for us not to stare.

In the rest of the world, the drinking age is eighteen. I had a giggle last night when I saw a Facebook post from a British friend who had just settled her son in university in the United Kingdom. Her post read, "Uni drop off is complete, he has his induction week timetable, beer in the fridge, and money in his wallet, my job is done." I laughed so hard as the Americanized part of me was shocked. Then I remembered my South-African side that celebrated my eighteenth birthday in a nightclub with a drink (or two).

Once on holiday and exploring Czechia on a warm summer's morning, we saw a mom with a toddler on her hip holding a beer. (It was summer in Europe; why wouldn't you have a beer in the morning?) The toddler reached for the beer mug, so the mom happily held it to her lips for her to drink. No problem; she was thirsty.

I share this with you not to change your views on alcohol or to convince anyone into letting minors drink. I share this as a reminder that there is more than one way to do almost everything. As you can see, other cultures do things differently. Seeing how others raise their children is always exciting to me. Throughout my travels, and while living in so many different countries, I have found that culture dictates how we raise children. And most importantly, I have learned that no one is ever wrong when it comes to parenting. Just different. I do not believe in changing how you parent either. I do, however, believe in acknowledging that others might be right, too.

## LESSONS LEARNED

- Child time. Family time. Adult time.

- The importance of time with your children and the importance of time without your children.

- Time without your children can also instill independence in them from a very early age.

- When we give our children time to learn how to be with other adults and time to develop their independence, they can become stronger.

- There are consequences for bad actions.

- Children should be able to speak to any adult comfortably.

- Children should understand the conduct expected in every environment.

- Parents need to clearly explain behavior expectations to children before any event.

- If you allow your kids to act as they wish in any environment, they will not learn to act as adults.

- No one acts as they want to whenever they want, so why would we let our children behave that way.

- There is more than one way to do almost everything.

- No one is ever really wrong when it comes to parenting. Just different.

CHAPTER 6

# ACKNOWLEDGING CHILDREN WITH SPECIAL NEEDS AND THEIR PARENTS

*"A child with special needs will inspire you
to be a special kind of person."*

*— Anonymous*

The Merriam-Webster Dictionary defines "special needs" as: any of various difficulties (such as a physical, emotional, behavioral, or learning disability or impairment) that causes an individual to require additional or specialized services or accommodations (such as in education or recreation).

In this chapter, we'll look at a few different types of special needs children and their parents. Parents are parents regardless. Every family looks different, has different needs, and is in a different place in their journey. Special needs families need more because they do more.

## DOWN SYNDROME

Here is a definition of Down syndrome I saw on a T-shirt:

Down syndrome
/doun sindrom/
Noun

1.  Genetic condition resulting from a third copy of the twenty-first chromosome.

2.  The innate ability to see the good and beauty in the world, to radiate joy and happiness, and to offer a unique perspective on life with the ability to change others' perceptions.

I decided to add this chapter after I was given a beautiful sign on a flight across Australia from Darwin to Sydney. As usual, the plane's bathroom line stretched past a few rows of seats. As I stood in the aisle, taking time to look at everyone sitting in their seats, a boy with Down syndrome caught my eye. He looked at me cautiously, so I gave him a friendly wave and a little smile. He waved back, then asked my name. We exchanged names, and then I began a polite conversation with him and his mom, asking if they were coming home or going on a holiday. What struck me was not this young boy with Down syndrome. His reaction to me is what I would have expected from a beautiful boy with Down syndrome. His mother's reaction was what struck me the most.

She was so happy I had taken the time to greet her son and not simply shy away. She soon started telling me about her son; she was so proud of him, and just like all parents, she wanted to share his amazing qualities. It was this pleasant, short interaction that motivated me to include this chapter because it taught me yet another massive lesson: All parents need to be acknowledged. Often, parents of children with special needs are not seen or heard. Most of us feel uncomfortable, not knowing how to act or what to say when we encounter a special needs child and parent. I know because that is exactly how I used to feel before I took the time to learn and simply start saying, "Hello." Before, when I would see a special needs child, I would think, *Could I ask questions?* I never thought the answer was yes, but you can ask questions. Yes, you can say, "Hello." Special needs parents love their children as much as you love yours; they want for them exactly what you want for yours. And they do not want you to feel guilty. Most just want to be acknowledged as a parent and not ignored.

During the first half of my adult life, I was a professional dancer and dance teacher. I loved it so much; I studied dance and theatre in college, earned my degree, and then moved into professional dance companies in South Africa and Europe for the next ten years. Yet, with decades of education, training, and experience as a dancer, dance teacher, and choreographer, I never learned how to ensure everyone could dance, not just the able-bodied. It was a long journey for me to learn and feel comfortable enough to begin teaching dance to children and young adults with Down syndrome, severe autism, and physical limitations. This journey changed me forever.

In 2010, I was teaching at an amazing dance school in Washington State call the Olympia Dance Center, a school that warmly welcomed anyone who wanted to dance. Each Saturday, I taught an open class for anyone to join in. One day, Dylan, a boy with Down syndrome, came to my lesson. He was so passionate about dance and was quite good, definitely good enough to keep up with the other students. However, Dylan had some "triggers" that would change him from a balanced, focused student to a disruptive one. Unfortunately, I had no idea how to handle his triggers. Weeks passed of him trying to work through the class, only to get triggered, while I didn't know what to do. He eventually stopped coming to my lessons. I completely failed him.

It was unacceptable to me that Dylan had stopped dancing there, but I had no idea how to include him in the class. I truly wished he had not left because of my inability to teach someone with Down syndrome, but

I had no one to turn to for advice or training. I was stuck in an uncomfortable, guilty place. I could not share my love of dance with everyone.

Life is funny. A year later, it was time to move again, and this time the Army moved us to England. Wouldn't you know it—a few miles from my house was an organization called Gloucestershire Dance (or Gdance) that specialized in inclusive dance. This dance company provided inclusive classes for all disabilities and able-bodied dancers. They believed everyone could dance, and no one should be left out. I offered myself as a volunteer teacher in exchange for training. I was determined to avoid failing another young person, and that is how my next life lesson began.

The first step was getting over my belief that only young, able, strong bodies could dance. I had to start looking at why people danced, not at their body composition and mobility to determine if they could. Often getting over our own beliefs is the hardest part about learning new lessons, and that was exactly where I was. Whether it is teaching dance or teaching your child a life lesson, you have to see the entire picture from all perspectives first, not just through your own lenses.

Gloucestershire Dance had all the teenagers in one class—some had Down syndrome, some were deaf, and some were in wheelchairs. They all danced because it felt good to them. Even if their dancing did not look the same, the effects were. Every student felt good. Dance forever changed for me during those months. One student, who was in a wheelchair, nonverbal, and fifteen years old, offered me the lesson of a lifetime and a glimpse into her life. She had an electric wheelchair, and our class was on the second floor of a building in the middle of a small city. She got to class each week all by herself, without the help of a parent or guardian. One day, I was so intrigued about how she did this that I followed her. Like a secret agent, I watched her leave the studio after class, get in the elevator, go out the doors, through a busy parking lot, onto the sidewalk (which was a good five-minute walk), then five blocks down the road, and to the main road. She crossed the street and waited at a bus stop in peak traffic. The bus arrived, the ramp went down, and she rolled on. I was dumbfounded. I stood there amazed at the effort it took her to come each week. Why did she make all this effort to come to a dance class? Especially when she was in a wheelchair, and all she could physically move were her arms. Why? It was there, on that street corner in busy Gloucestershire's city center that I realized we all share the same human desires and feelings.

On another occasion, I met a boy named Daniel. Once a week, I would set classes on a special theme. Each week, we would teach the children a combination and add one step to the final dance. Daniel had severe autism, so severe he could not connect with anyone. He never made eye contact and was solely focused in his own small world—until one day, he connected!

Luckily, on that day, his parents came to watch him in class because, at one point, Daniel slowly looked around for his parents, found them in the corner watching intently, stared them in the eye, and danced! He was smiling, laughing, and doing all the steps we had taught him the previous weeks. He connected with his mama to share his joy. Daniel was having fun, and his mother could see it, and more importantly, share it with him. It was truly a special parenting moment.

The tears still flow as I write this because that had to be one of the worthiest times of my whole life. I got to see it, and more than anything else, I got to feel it. His mom was a crying mess along with his teachers and the rest of us. From that moment on, I knew I would give my time freely to ensure I could be a part of these very special people and their very special parents' lives. At that very moment, I changed my perception and saw a bit more of the world as a parent. I believe children with special needs, including those with Down syndrome and all the others, were put on the earth to teach us all a little something. The problem is most people do not stop to hear the lesson they have to share.

Fast forward five years and two more military moves—I had another opportunity to learn a life lesson from special needs children and parents. I was living in Virginia, where I got to work with another fantastic organization in Norfolk called "MixMo" (Mixed Abilities in Motion). This was run with the help of a team of volunteers, who built the most incredible community. MixMo taught a mixed abilities dance class at eight on Saturday mornings. This was a super-fun class that brightened up everyone's weekend. MixMo had both volunteers and professionals from fifteen to fifty years old. It was a buzzing hive of parents, siblings, musicians, doctors, and teachers, all coming together to help teach dance to some very special people. People with Down syndrome from three- to forty-two-years-old participated in three classes, each set to their age group or ability level.

During these unique classes, I learned six important lessons:

1. **To let go of the ego:** Special needs children genuinely do not care what others think about them. They live by the credo, "Dance like no one's watching." If we could harness even a bit of this superpower, I bet we would all be much happier. Imagine if you could let go of your ego.

2. **To love freely:** Many special needs children look you in your eyes without judgment—no preconceived ideas of who you are—then give you a big hug. They do not hide love, control it, or hand it out in little bits. They express it as it flows out of them. Imagine if we could love freely.

3. **To own it:** If a special needs child does something and you praise them for their good job, a normal response might be, "I know." They own the great job they've done. For them, the "doing" is their focus, not what others think of how they did it. Imagine if we could own it.

4. **Give yourself what you need:** They give themselves what they need when they need it. If they need a break, they take it; if they

need to do double what was asked, they do it. Imagine if you gave yourself what you needed.

5. **Give real greetings:** Saying hello and goodbye to the children was my favorite part of my Saturdays at MixMo. Each hello and goodbye was so heartfelt, so genuine, and so open. Each one was an event. Imagine if we could make a greeting the highlight of someone's day.

6. **Celebrate every victory:** Nothing is too big or too small to warrant a high-five (to everyone in the room), a happy dance, a big hug, or a precious nose-to-nose moment.

Imagine if we could celebrate every victory. How free would we all be? I walked out of class each Saturday morning feeling like a fraud to say I taught them. Those very special children were the real teachers.

And even though I feel like I failed Dylan years before in Washington, I think the gift, in the end, was for me to start my journey to actually learning from special needs children.

When you see a child with any special need, or a family with a special need, don't ignore them. Simply say, "Hello." I promise you will walk away from the interaction feeling a special kind of love.

I once held a mom while she cried after buying her three-year-old with Down syndrome a pair of ballet shoes. She told me she had danced as a child and always dreamt of taking her daughter to dance class to experience the magic she had. Once she found out her daughter had Down syndrome, she spent years changing her vision for her child. She said she thought she had to let that dream go. But on that day, she was able to buy her daughter her first pair of ballet shoes. She cried because she now saw the dream did not have to be dissolved; it just needed to be adapted a little. She changed her parenting perception to see a more complete picture, not just the view from her past experience. We all have dreams and wishes for our children, and the parents who care for these special people need our support. Even a warm smile can provide ease on a hard day. Our village, the parenting village, needs to spread out to all parents because we all need a little more kindness and support.

## PARENTS OF CHILDREN WITH SPECIAL NEEDS

My friend Patricia is an advocate for children with autism. Patricia supports families with autistic children in Canberra, Australia, by going into a family's home and helping the whole family adapt and thrive in their unique environment. I felt Patricia needed to be in this book to give a voice to parents of children with autism, and also to help those who have friends, family, or colleagues with children somewhere on the spectrum to understand a bit more. Patricia is an expert. I merely sit and listen to her stories in awe of what it looks like to make a difference in people's lives.

Patricia and I meet for coffee once a month—an event I look forward to because I always walk away better than when I arrived. Our last meetup was in a busy metropolitan coffee shop. There she told me a bit more about autism and how it affects people throughout their lives.

The biggest lesson Patricia taught me was that autism is not necessarily increasing in the world; professionals are just getting better at diagnosing it. That is fantastic because children who used to slip between the cracks are now getting the support and help they need.

Sometimes, you cannot tell if a child is on the spectrum. Patricia explained that when you live with an autistic child, you can see it more easily. But people who do not share the child's private space cannot. This makes it very difficult for the average person to identify an autistic child or to understand how the parents are trying to parent in a very different environment than most.

Patricia told me a story about one of her clients who was getting ice cream from an ice-cream van for her two children. The older child had autism and was around eight or nine. While in line, the child had a meltdown. The poor mom was dealing with this as best as she could when another mom ahead of them in the line thought it was necessary to give her opinion by saying, "I think someone has lost their ice cream privilege today." The autistic child's six-year-old sister came to the rescue by stating her brother had autism and still deserved his ice cream. The snarky, judgmental mom just looked at the family and walked away, embarrassed.

This story teaches a lesson we can all learn. We have no idea what is actually going on in anyone's family. Not a clue. A better, kinder, more reasonable response to this situation would have been for the snarky woman to help the mom and be supportive. Maybe pass a kind word about how well she was doing in the day-to-day parenting struggles, or at least a smile…anything. Parents need to give parents a break, not judgment.

The sad part is the judgmental mom's son was watching the judging and will most likely continue the judgment cycle when he becomes a father. What a lost opportunity for the parent to teach compassion and kindness instead of judgment. There are opportunities every-where to teach our children. We just have to see parenting from dif-ferent perspectives.

## PARENTING WITH AN ASPERGER'S CHILD

Jennifer, a great friend of mine from Washington State, is one tough cookie and an incredibly special woman who cares about everyone she meets. She is the parent of a child with Asperger's. When you hear how other parents have treated her over the years, you will un-derstand why she has developed a thick skin and why she is one of the most gracious women I know. When she told me this very per-sonal parenting story one morning at her kitchen table where we would gather regularly, I was absolutely shocked. At that point in my parenting journey, I didn't know there were parents and people in the world who would be purposefully mean to other moms.

Jenn has two boys—her oldest is a wonderful, smart, and funny, totally self-sufficient twenty-one-year-old right now. He has Asperger's. His success in life has a lot to do with Jennifer and her husband's commitment to him as parents. Children with Asperger's have difficulties with social development and can be nonverbal for a while or even forever. They can have restricted and repetitive patterns of behaviors and get overwhelmed and overstimulated very easily. Jenn's son would open and close a door for ages as a child. Open, close, open, close, until his need to do this burnt itself out. This type of behavior could happen anywhere, and as Jenn learned, not everyone around her understood what was happening and very few were gracious about the situation. If her son was stopped in the middle of his opening, closing behavior, he would have a meltdown. People would shout at her, telling her to "stop him" or "deal with him." These people (usually other parents) didn't know or understand that she was not unable to control her son; she was merely figuring out day to day how to help and support him. And to make it worse, this was her first child, and she was learning like we all learn with our firsts, but with many more issues to deal with.

When Jenn took her family to Disneyland on what they hoped would be a magical experience, she applied for disabled family passes. These special passes would help Jen and her husband keep their son in a calmer and more controlled environment throughout the park and not have to wait in lines for hours at a time, where he would surely get overwhelmed by the noise, people, and movement. Quieter lines were what Jenn needed to help her son enjoy the magic of Disney. But, unfortunately, even in "the happiest place on earth," other parents would call her out because her son did not look like he had a disability.

Not all disabilities are visible. Jenn explained that, in most lines, she had to calmly tell everyone why they were there. She said she was always educating people about her son and their situation; it was a never-ending, uphill battle against other parents. There is no reason such a wonderful person, trying to do her best as a parent, should have had to deal with this, especially at the happiest place on earth.

Sometimes on the playground, parents would ask her to leave because they found her two-year old's behavior unacceptable or inappropriate. No questions asked, no concern for another parent; they just thought he was a spoiled brat and should not be around their "better behaved children."

After telling her parenting stories, Jennifer left me with this bombshell statement: "Unless I see another parent in the corner smoking crack next to their child, I will assume they are doing their best."

I share this story to highlight how one mean look or negative comment can accumulate over a special needs parent's life. The best option for us all to follow is to be tolerant, understanding, and kind. Even the smallest demonstration of support or act of kindness toward a special needs parent's difficult circumstances could brighten their entire day.

Take some time now to think about situations similar to the preceding stories. Write down what you don't understand and would like to learn more about. This will help you understand more fully and be more supportive to other parents.

_____

_____

_____

_____

_____

_____

_____

_____

### LESSONS LEARNED

- Working from a place of understanding always takes more effort, but it is beneficial to everyone involved.

- Move away from the easy wrong toward the hard right, mentality.

- Make the effort to ask uncomfortable questions, smile, and be helpful—it's so much more rewarding and therapeutic than living in the judgmental mind.

- Do not jump to quick judgment; you probably don't know what is going on.

# CHAPTER 7

# PARENTING IN 'STRAYA (AUSTRALIA)

*"We are all visitors to this time, this place—we are just passing through. Our purpose here is to observe, to learn, to grow, to love, and then we return home."*

*— Aboriginal Proverb*

Learning Australian lingo (language) is a fair dinkum (excellent) experience. Most friendships are born around a cuppa (a cup of coffee). It's easy to find mates (friends) as people are defo (definitely friendly). Their schedules are choc a block (full), as they are as flat out like a lizard drinking (very busy), but there is always time for a brekky (breakfast).

Culture in Australia is strong, rough, and rugged. Moving here from the United States, southern Virginia specifically, was a culture shock for sure. No more, "Hey, sweeties," when you walked into a store or "Hey, darling," and "Welcome, y'all." In Australia, everyone is a "mate," and it is wonderful.

## CROCODILE DANI

Cooee!

*A loud, Aboriginal cry in the "outback" that tells people where you are, assuming they are within cooee range. If you're not within a cooee of something, you're nowhere bloody near it.*

During one Australian winter (June, July, and August), our family decided to head to the Outback for some warmth and culture. We were living in the capital city of Canberra, in Southern Australia, where winter is definitely cold—in the Northern Territory, temperatures would reach ninety degrees Fahrenheit on a winter's day. We wanted to experience the Australian outback and all its amazing offerings. Living in Canberra felt like Australia, but did not reflect the whole country, and definitely, was not like the Australia we thought we knew from Hollywood movies. Taking recommendations from our local friends (locals always know the best places to visit on holiday), we decided to go to the top of the country, to Kakadu National Park.

The trip from Canberra to Darwin was a six-hour flight plus a two-and-a-half-hour drive to our campsite, which was in the middle of nowhere. There was no internet, TV, or even a trace of cellphone signal. We were absolutely in the boonies. Coeee! Silence…. No one was bloody near us!

Upon arrival at the camp, a staff member briefed us about all the things that could kill us in the area. Crocodiles had been the most significant issue in the past. There was a billabong (large pond or lake) about half a mile away, but the staff did not expect crocodiles to make their way to camp this time of year. There were 22,000 crocodiles in this part of Australia alone. Another concern was walking at night. The camp staff insisted everyone use a torch (flashlight); otherwise, we were very likely to step on a snake. We were asked to sign a form saying we understood the dangers and would not hold the camp accountable if anything happened. No swimming anywhere at any time. Torch at night. Got it! So, on that warm fuzzy note, we started planning our next few days.

Using our rental car, a four-by-four truck, of course, we went driving and landed in Jabiru, the smallest town I have ever seen. By the looks of the town and the locals, there was no preponderance of wealth, just an air of roughness. But it was not the lack of wealth that seemed to bring out the roughness. In South Africa, I had grown up around and seen the effects of extreme poverty, but here it was different. I did not understand what this feeling was.

While in the town, I noticed someone had rubbed mud in a line, about chest high, all over the buildings. It looked as if it had just been smeared on by hand—layers and layers of mud, all in a line around most of the buildings in the small shopping area. Wondering what it was, I approached two Aboriginal women. I politely asked them what the mud was all about. They stared at me silently for a while; then one laughed. The other dismissively said, "It's for a funeral," and walked away. That's all I got. (I later learned the mud smears were part of the "sorry ritual," where the deceased's energy needs to be removed from every place they ever went; this could sometimes take years.) I could not understand why they had been dismissive to me or why they laughed at me. Then, walking back to my car, I noticed that no Aboriginal person even looked at us as we went by. It was like we were ghosts.

The next day, we booked a private tour with a guide to ensure we saw the most significant areas of this very large national park and could learn more about the culture. We knew someone would collect us and take us for the whole day in the Outback. I was not sure where we were going, but we were excited. That morning, an older, well-worn white woman arrived at the camp and found us at breakfast. I guess I was expecting an Aboriginal man, so I was a bit thrown back. Introducing herself as Dani, she announced we were leaving and walked toward the truck. I felt like I was talking to those same two aboriginal women, which made me feel cautious toward Dani. What was I doing to cause this kind of harsh reaction from the locals? Dani seemed harder than I had ever felt a woman to be—abrasive and bordering on mean.

After driving for an hour on dirt roads and still in the middle of nowhere, which was beautiful as could be, but still in the middle of nowhere, Dani took us to our first stop, her childhood home. She took time to describe her life growing up in the Outback and all that came with it. It was then I realized why she was so hard. She had to be.

Dani was a white woman whose mother had left her at age two. Her father remarried an Aboriginal woman, and they started a family. Dani was initiated into an Aboriginal tribe at the age of two and was brought up as an Aboriginal by a woman she described as the most incredible person, a person she soon called mother. Her father was a crocodile farmer, and as a family, they bred, rescued, and cared for crocodiles. Their house was built from termite mounds, a hardened mud, nearly cement-like ironwood posts, and corrugated metal siding. As the day went on, and Dani could see our family was truly interested in her culture and the Outback, she began to open up more, telling us how she had nine brothers and sisters. Three of them were sadly taken from the family by the Australian government and were among the Stolen Children.

Back story: From 1910 to the 1970s, indigenous children (Aboriginals) were removed from their families as part of the policy of assimilation. The Australian government believed children would be more adaptable to learning white ways than adults would be. The idea was that all Aboriginal people would "die out" and be assimilated into white culture and communities. The children were made to reject their heritage and not use their traditional languages; in fact, these languages were forbidden. Children who had an Aboriginal and white parentage mix were extremely vulnerable to removal. These children are known as "Stolen Children."

Dani's young brothers and sisters fell into the category of the vulnerable group and were taken from the family when they were two, four, and five years old. That story hit me like a ton of bricks. The Aboriginal women I spoke to in Jabiru could have or must have been affected by this horrific time in history. No wonder they wanted nothing to do with a white woman. I represented nothing but pain to them.

Dani then told us how she raised her three children in the Outback, learning both aboriginal and white ways. By this time, I had softened to Dani because I could see life more clearly from her perspective. Later in the day, we went on a short hike to a cave complex. Just before arriving, she stopped us and pulled out a ten-inch knife, saying, "There was a boar around here yesterday and a croc made its way from the river last week. Stay behind me, and stay alert." It was like a scene out of *Crocodile Dundee* (the 1986 film, which is very true to the Australian Outback). Luckily, we did not come across any boars or crocs. But if we did, I knew Dani would take care of it. By this point, I had become very impressed by her strength, courage, and life. Perspective changes everything.

After our hike, we made our way to Ubirr, one of the most beautiful places in Kakadu. We hiked in, climbing rocks and boulders, and looking at the Aboriginal art on the side of the rocks. Dani explained that one particular area, near a huge rock face and boulders placed perfectly for seats, is where all the Aboriginal kids in the area come to learn about their history. The rock art showed the lessons of culture and the "ten commandments" that all Aboriginal children had to learn. The Aboriginal Ten Commandments, or lessons, covered laws regarding homicide, sacrilege, sorcery, incest, abduction of women, adultery, physical assault, theft, and insult, including swearing. The area looked just like an outdoor classroom. So we all sat in this "school" and listened to Dani's stories about Aboriginal history and culture. It reminded me of how we are all ancestors of storytellers, and our love for stories is generational.

One of those Aboriginal stories was about Mabuyu, a tale to teach everyone not to steal. The tale goes like this:

Mabuyu was a giant and one of the caretakers of the Aboriginal lands. He went fishing every day for his food, and each time on his way back to his tribe, some youngsters would steal his fish. He finally got fed up with their stealing, so he decided to teach them a lesson. One day he was dragging his catch on a string after a fishing expedition when the youngsters stole his fish. That night, Mabuyu waited until the young thieves had eaten his fish and were camped inside their cave near the East Alligator River. Once the youngsters were asleep, he blocked the mouth of the cave with a huge rock. The next morning when they woke, they could not come out of the cave. The youngsters were never seen again.

The Mabuyu lesson—because the youngsters stole, they got punished. The story was a lesson in both stealing and showing there are consequences to your actions.

Dani shared many stories like this. Most were similar to Western commandments, but they all had some magic or folklore intricately weaved into them. Sitting there on the rocks, staring at the rock art on the gigantic boulder in front of me, and listening to Dani tell her stories, I could see how this type of teaching through storytelling could influence a child. Children can remember the smallest detail of every story they have ever heard or seen. So why not teach life lessons through stories? It worked for the Aboriginal tribes.

While Dani was telling the stories, my son saw a stick laying near a eucalyptus tree. Like most little boys would, he picked up a stick and started breaking it. Dani went up to him immediately, and with her strong spirit, told him he must put the stick down. She explained that nature put the stick there for a reason, and "If everyone moved nature whenever they wanted to, nature would, over time, become unbalanced." This one little lesson from the Outback was truly profound for our entire family. I had never considered this the way Dani explained it. Especially now, with the state of our planet, her explanation was perfect and completely relatable to everyone in the family. My son stood there, contemplating the enormity of her words. He put the stick down slowly and thoughtfully, as he (and all of us) considered how true her words were.

Dani's Aboriginal and life stories drove me to ask more questions about her culture, a culture considered primitive by many throughout history. But did the Aboriginals have it right the whole time? I asked Dani about how they see other cultures. Do the Aboriginals only welcome fellow Aboriginals into their community, and how did they accept her and her father? She said, "We believe everyone should help each other; we should all be useful like the birds are to one another. No matter what species they are, they all work as one. Human, animal, bird, and fish are a part of one large, unchanging network of relationships that can be traced to the Great Spirit ancestors. We all should work together, and humans should work even harder for the earth." Dani went on to explain that, in nature, each species of plant and animal has a purpose that helps the others. "Humans have no purpose on this planet. We are not needed here, so for that reason, we should work harder to serve it."

By the end of the day, and after many questions to try to understand Dani and her culture, I left in total awe of her and her life. My daughter said to me, "Well, I have a new role model." My sense that we can all better understand others by simply asking questions about their lives and then asking more questions was renewed. People are not just going to open up their lives for you to look at; you need to ask more lovingly: Why? How? Then what happened? How did that affect you?

Dani's life was a few lives all wrapped into one, and the lessons she delivered through stories and a wonderful Australian strength will stay with me forever. How are we serving others? How are we serving the planet? How are we teaching our children?

## BUILDING AN ENDOSKELETON

My business allows me to meet wonderful people all over the world, in part, through personal interactions and networking events. It seems like every networking event is filled with interesting and creative people. They are kind of like buffets of personalities, cultures, and experiences, with each person having a different story to tell. During one of these events, I met an inspiring woman named Wendy. We got to chatting, and she had a fascinating story that I thankfully retell here.

Wendy and her husband Patrick were missionaries throughout the world, which allowed her to raise her family in multiple countries through their childhood and teenage years. Meeting this unique woman, who had basically lived my life of travel already, opened an opportunity for me to ask her questions and explore her life more deeply.

Wendy's children were in their late twenties and thirties, and she was a grandmother of four, but she was still full of energy, almost like she was still in her twenties. She had so much energy, in fact, that she started a new business in her sixties when most people were trying to stop working. She has a beautiful relationship with her adult children and her grandbabies. She takes her grandchildren skiing, teaches them about life, and is not afraid to discipline them as a grandmother. Wendy's life story was one of highs and lows, heartache and triumph, despite all the moves and inconsistency the missionary life brings. She was so awesome, in fact, that I actually told her I wanted to be her when I grew up.

One morning over coffee, I finally asked Wendy if her adult kids benefitted from moving around so much, or did all the moves hurt them in some way. Her answer was so powerful that it changed my perspective right there and then on how I raise my own children.

Wendy explained, from her experience as a missionary and traveling the world, that some people get too fixated on giving their children a stable environment and forget to actually "build" the child. When moving around from city to city and country to country, you can only focus on the child's inner strength since there is very little else to hold on to. She expanded further, "Think of building a child from the inside out, not the outside in.

You either raise a child with an endoskeleton or an exoskeleton."

Brilliant! I loved that analogy. It says so much so simply. We, as parents, need to "build" our little humans, soon to be big humans, from the inside out, not the outside in. A "village" of consistent family members, friends, teachers, preachers, pastors, and coaches is a tremendous asset to surround your child with, and it is tremendously helpful to you as a parent. (I am secretly jealous of those who have a constant village around them.) It can provide differing perspectives and lessons (stories) about life. But sometimes, we can rely too much on that village and forget it is our job as parents to build our children. Others can assist and provide a second and third backup if needed. I don't believe for a second that raising children falls completely on parents' shoulders, but we are primarily responsible.

Having an active village or community is a great asset that helps build your child's exoskeleton. This happens year in and year out through life's interactions in their village and experiences gained. However, what happens at home, during personal, intimate times with parents, builds the endoskeleton. You may wonder what happens in the quiet moments in the home at bedtime, dinner, or the breakfast table, around meal preparation, and my all-time favorite, driving. In all those places, so many opportunities exist to build our children's endoskeletons, simply by listening to what they are saying and then applying life lessons to their day-to-day experiences. We can engage with our children over and over (and over) again about the same issues when they arise year after year. That type of consistency and effort is what builds a strong endoskeleton. The most powerful life lessons come from parents through our own experiences and stories shared with our children.

These opportunities, however, must be fashioned into our daily lives. They do not always magically appear out of thin air. Well, sometimes they do, and when that happens, we should take the time to act there and then. We, as parents, can build time or opportunities in our normal lives to find magic moments that build the endoskeleton. These magic moments can appear anywhere and at any time: After a movie, by discussing the moral of a story. After school pickup, by asking about their day. When you get home from work, by asking about the games they played at day care. While they are doing homework. While you are cooking dinner. Literally, anywhere. But let's not rely on them. It is better to build a magic hour or moment into our everyday life. Meals are a great time to get deep and personal. In the car, your kids are literally trapped in a small room with you. Perfect!

Locations are key, but timing is everything for a magic hour or moment. Your children cannot be tired or distracted. No magic happens then. We are looking for times when the kids are calm and when their energy and patience are at their best. Evenings, for me, are often not the best time because my kids are always tired after school. If they have after school activities and sport practices, they come home exhausted and have not yet processed everything that happened in their day. I personally build a magic hour (well half hour) into breakfast. Every morning, I make a big breakfast, sit the kids down at the table, eat, and chat. If Deric is available, he joins us as well. That is when everything comes pouring out of the kids. They are fresh, rested, ready for a new day, and super-chatty.

Now you may be thinking, *How in the hell do you do that in the morning? I am rushing around trying to get everyone out the door on time!* I have to plan ahead to include that time in our daily schedule. That means I get up an hour earlier to make breakfast and prep, then wake the kids up thirty minutes earlier than they actually need to be up. But before I can do all that, I have to get the kids to bed earlier the night before to ensure they get the rest they need to be fresh in the morning. *I build time into my day to facilitate child-to-parent interactions under the best conditions.* Of course, this does not happen every day of every month of every year. Life can sometimes get messy, and it's guaranteed Murphy will step in to challenge us, but this time is important to us, so we do everything in our power to preserve it.

When are your family's *magic hours*? Are they in the morning? At dinner time? On car rides? Weekends? There are no wrong answers. Think about quality over quantity.

_____

_____

_____

_____

_____

_____

_____

_____

Don't have any yet? No worries! When might you build some magic moments into your day?

_____

_____

_____

_____

_____

_____

_____

## NO WORRIES, MATE; SHE'LL BE RIGHT!

"She'll be right" is a very common Aussie saying. Basically, it means everything will be okay or all right. The wonderful (and quite contagious) laid-back atmosphere of Australia is built deep into the culture. If your child misses a shot on goal in a soccer game, parents shout from the sideline, "Unlucky, mate." No stress, no worries; everything will be all right; just move on. What a remarkable way to keep stress out of a game and focus on the fun!

I like this attitude because, as the kids come off the field, they have very little anxiety about making mistakes or messing up in the game—she'll be right; no worries. Most parents stand on the side of the sports field quietly and calmly, chatting among themselves. They might have a cuppa for morning rugby matches or a glass of wine or a beer at a cricket match. (Yep...a glass of wine or two at a grade school cricket match!) No insistent yelling or screaming at their kids, coaches, or referees. Some of the coaches do not even shout; they just let the kids go out on their own and figure it out as a team, then have a chat with them at halftime. This kind of sporting experience was completely different from the more aggressive American (and me shouting on the sidelines) style of youth sports I experienced.

The best part about Australian youth sports was the sausage sizzle. At nearly every sporting event, you can get a sausage sizzle. This is an Australian sausage (kind of like a German bratwurst and American hotdog mixed...but completely different) on a slice of white bread, usually served with grilled onions and tomato sauce (ketchup). On a cold morning at a sports event, you can often find a dad grilling some bacon and eggs to put on a roll. It is simple. And that, my friend, is the important part. Australians seem to simplify things. No food handler's course required to cook at events. No rule that only store-bought products are allowed at school. There were tween girls, mine included, helping out with no issues. Everything was relaxed and without worry.

Maybe that is why nearly everyone in Australia says "no worries"—because they actually mean it, and they are literally not worried. *No worries equals no stress.* If we could apply just a small portion of this Australian mindset to our parenting, our children might just grow without the stressors that adults and parents put on them so often. "Do well in school. Get good grades. Play sports. Win every game. Be the team captain. Get an athletic scholarship. Play an instrument. Be in the band. Be in a social club. Create a club. Go to church. Be an Eagle Scout. Get into the best college.

Holy moly, I'm stressed just writing all that.

Now, don't get me wrong. I think competition is healthy, and I do want my children to do well in school and sports and get into a good college. But if our children do not get perfect grades and are not the team captain, that doesn't mean they will be unsuccessful.

Academic and athletic success *absolutely do not* mean our children will be happy.

So, what do we really want for our children? To be happy, healthy, financially secure adults who contribute positively to their communities. That's about it. I am not convinced that we, as parents, should be adding so many additional stressors to our children's lives, pushing them to excel in everything they do. First, it is impossible. Second, it just doesn't matter that much in the big picture. Not everyone is athletically inclined or physically built to be a college or professional athlete. Not everyone can be a computer scientist or doctor who saves the world. I truly believe the Aussies have a good thing going on—no worries, mate. She'll be right.

Australians, thankfully, are not relaxed about their coffee. They take their coffee very seriously—they expect excellent coffee. Even at youth sports events, there is a coffee van, which is set up by a barista in a mobile coffee shop. No drip coffee. Flat whites. Cappuccinos. Espressos only. Which, by the way, I do support. Thanks for the cuppa!

## SHUT THE FRONT DOOR!

What was shocking for my family on arrival in Australia was the swearing. Yes, I said swearing. On our arrival, I was warned by a few non-Australians that the Aussies swear a lot. "Make sure your children are prepared for what they will hear at school," a woman warned me. (My kids were nine and eleven at the time.) "Children here use the worst language you will ever hear." O-K-A-Y...I got it. Not entirely sure what to expect, I took a wait-and-see attitude. *Every culture is different,* I thought to myself. However, I soon understood why we received so many warnings from non-Australians.

Yes, more "bad" language is spoken regularly in Australia than anywhere else I have lived. It was comical at times from our limited point of view. The "forbidden words" were thrown around liberally on TV, on the radio, walking down the street, and in the mall. High schoolers at rugby matches shouted and, I'm not kidding, sung the off-limits words to the opposing team. It was so far beyond our view of appropriate speech, it was actually hilarious.

What could we do? Nothing but laugh. The kids eventually found the swearing to be a funny cultural twist they loved to report on at breakfast every morning. After about a month, we did not hear about it anymore since the initial shock wore off and harsher language became normal. One day Devin said, "So, let me get this straight, someone makes up a word and labels it a *bad* word; then forevermore, it is off-limits and banned for all to use it?"

"Yep," I replied.

"But it's just a word or a bunch of sounds," my son replied.

The beauty of this situation is that cursing does not seem to faze Aussies. They have had the shock factor removed from taboo words. No one cares. Now, I am not saying parents should teach forbidden words to two years old, but cultures and adults give words their weight, deeming them "good" or "bad." I'm not proud to say the kids might have heard their first curse words from me. (I had a side bet with Deric it was going to be him. He is in the Army.) Seeing the relaxed culture around swearing firsthand put the whole bad language thing in a different perspective. Plus, now I don't feel so bad about losing the swearing bet to my husband.

At a conference I attended in an upmarket, beautiful hotel in Canberra, the super-cool, super-vibrant Australian keynote speaker began her opening remarks by putting $50 in her swear jar to cover all the F-bombs she was about to drop. By the end of the talk, everyone agreed she owed the jar some more money. But boy, was it ever effective! I listened intently the whole afternoon.

On the opposite side of the spectrum is my very dear friend Allison. She has never used a swear word in her life. Not one. She made that decision as a young adult and has remained true to her word. She does not care if anyone around her swears; it is just her personal choice not to, and I respect her decision and self-control immensely. But in Australia, parents can swear happily and then follow it up with, "She'll be right." When we make a big deal out of something, it becomes a big deal. When we don't, it does not. So, what are we making a big deal of? What is actually important in your and your children's lives? And just as important, how and when are you going to teach this to your children?

Around the world, cultures determine what is appropriate, and it is different everywhere. But parents can determine what is important just as well, despite the culture surrounding them.

What is truly important to your family?

_____

_____

_____

_____

_____

_____

_____


How are you going to teach what is important to your children?

_____

_____

_____

_____

_____

_____

_____

What are your family's non-negotiables—those rules or expectations that will not falter? Examples: no drinking and driving, no cursing, no using the Lord's name in vain, no bullying.

_____

_____

_____

_____

_____

_____

## LESSONS LEARNED

- Try to teach life lessons through stories. Children will remember this way—the Aboriginal way.

- Build your child from the inside out.

- Build an endoskeleton during those magic moments.

- Build time into the day to facilitate child-to-parent interactions under the right conditions.

- No worries, mate. She'll be right.

- When we make a big deal out of something, it becomes a big deal.

- Determine what is truly important to your family and figure out how you will teach it to your children.

CHAPTER 8

# TAKING TIME OUT FOR YOURSELF

*"I know God would not give me anything I can't handle;*
*I just wish God would not trust me so much."*

— *Mother Teresa*

The question I get asked more than any other is: "What is the best country or place you have ever lived in?" If there is one thing I have learned during our many moves, it is that no place (country, state, neighborhood) is perfect. It took me a while to see it, but no one place is truly perfect. No parent, or parenting situation, is perfect either. Here I am writing on a laptop that has no touchpad clicker because my son smashed it too hard when playing computer games, and now it is broken and unfixable. I still have gratitude for this mess of a computer because it is an upgrade to the last one I had, where my daughter pulled all the keys off when she was two because she thought it looked like a puzzle! Like I said, parenting is never perfect.

Another big lesson I have learned is everyone must rest—parents and children. Push forward, thrive, strive, accomplish, but then rest. It is in rest that we rebuild, renew, and reenergize. It is where we stop to listen, and where we can stop and hear. I was told by Hawaiian friend Rose when I had my firstborn to always respect both my baby's and my need for sleep. I love the way that sounds. Children need rest as much as they need food, love, and cuddles. We rest in order to handle the difficulties of parenting and life. We must rest.

## TAKE TIME FOR YOURSELF

Do you feel rested and calm as a parent?

Ha, that was a joke!

We all know that life with a newborn baby is not kind to our sleep needs. To anyone reading this book with a newborn…well, first, why are you reading now and not sleeping? Second, this phase will end. Even though you find yourself in the realization of what 24/7 actually means, know that this period in your life will end soon.

As parents, we need to respect children's sleep no matter their age. When I was teaching in a high school, I'd ask the teenagers when they went to bed. The average time was between 11 p.m. and 2 a.m. Even high schoolers are growing and need rest. A Chinese doctor I did a course with explained that Chinese medicine believes you cannot catch up on sleep. Once you miss a night's sleep, you cannot get it back. It is not a bank where you can withdraw and deposit as you need. It is a part of being human you can't ignore.

Respect your children's need for sleep, but don't forget to also respect your own. You are no good to anyone if you are always tired, drained, and living in a state of continual exhaustion. In that state, we are usually emotional, easily irritated, snappy, and often make bad decisions. We all know and understand as parents that there are times in your journey (usually with newborns) when you feel like you are always awake. These periods are usually short in duration (days, weeks, months), but could last years if you have children with special needs. Regardless of the duration, when you can rest, please rest! Sometimes you must literally "find" the time. When your baby or child sleeps, you sleep. When your toddler naps, you nap. Let your home stay messy for a while. Your rest is more important than the dishes getting cleaned. The baby doesn't care if the laundry is folded. Your baby, and your family for that matter, only care that you are rested because you are a better parent then. Rest is so critical to your emotional state as a parent. Parenting is hard…but it's harder when you're tired! Find time to rest.

When my first baby was only six weeks old, my husband was deployed to the war in Afghanistan. It would be his second war zone deployment, but our first as a couple and my first as a mother. I was all alone. The enormity of parenting hit me when I realized I had to keep this little human alive all by myself. (I could not even keep a houseplant alive, so how was I going to keep a baby alive?) One tired afternoon, I was invited to a friend's house for dinner. Invitations like this were something I never declined because it was an opportunity to eat with two hands and have an adult conversation. My friend Oriana was my rock and my complete support during this time. She was more experienced at parenting while I was still figuring everything out. Her mother, Aida, a woman who had a strong and quiet strength to her, was visiting from the Dominican Republic and joined us for dinner. As we sat down to eat a wonderful Dominican dinner, my daughter started fussing. I could not believe it. I was so hungry (I could not remember the last time I'd had a proper meal), and the food looked and smelled amazing. I not so calmly excused myself from the table and told Oriana and her mother I was going to feed the baby first; then I would join them again for dinner. Oriana's mom said, "No! The baby must wait. You eat before the baby." Shock! Horror! I did not know what to say. Put myself first? What craziness was this?

Taking care of myself was not what I had been taught in the hospital's baby classes or by all the baby books I had read. Surely my only role in this life from here on out was complete and all-encompassing care for this little human while forgoing all of my own needs and feelings. The lesson I received during that dinner was loud and clear. Parents have to make sure we are fine first. To be completely honest, it took me a few years to implement that very wise Dominican parenting lesson, but regardless of how many times I had to hit rock bottom, I finally saw what she was saying. I had to be okay, and I was the only one who had the power to put me on the list too.

## PARENTING ANXIETY

Fast forward two years to Deric's third, twelve-month combat deployment, this time to Iraq. I had a two-year-old toddler and a six-month-old baby, and I was in a new state, in a foreign country, with no family nearby. That's when I realized I couldn't keep going alone. (When you don't listen, life has a way to make you hear.)

With two small children and a husband in a war zone, I developed some crazy anxiety. I am not alone; many parents I meet have gone through this. The anxiety is hidden well, never discussed, but it seems to be everywhere in the parenting world. It's not unusual for friends to call me a few months after giving birth who have gone from powerful CEO to anxious, worried woman who panics every time the phone rings. The part that upsets me most is that parents seem to believe that after their children are born, life will be rainbows and unicorns. We seem to believe we will instantly know our children's every need and desire, and understand every part of this very small, very dependent human in our care. The truth is it seldom feels like that. In fact, not only are you learning a whole new person, but you are relearning a whole new you. When a baby is born, so is Mom and/or Dad, and they are entirely new people. The worst part is the new person you are trying to understand usually has not showered in days, is always hungry, and is constantly fuzzy and tired. So, typically, this "new you" is not the most appealing person. My grandmother used to say, "It is cruel of God to give a mom her first child first."

I think all birthing classes or baby books should teach moms about the changes that may occur in them too. We seem to be left to figure it out on our own, and most of the time, we end up feeling like failures. A friend who had older kids, about five- and eight-years-old, popped over to my house one time when I had two kids under two. She looked around and said, "Yep, looks like the house of a mom with two under two." I was mortified. Until that moment, I had not even looked at the house. And in that sentence, I looked around and saw what she meant. It looked like a hurricane had hit my kitchen and living room. The house did not represent who I was—well, who I thought I was anyway. (Who was I?) Truth be known, I should have just let it go and understood it was okay, that it was how it was right then, with no further expectations of myself.

But I didn't.

In that moment, I failed to remember to take care of myself first; I failed to remember to rest, and I started cleaning up the house.

The anxiety began slowly and crept up with such slyness that most of the time I did not see it coming. All of a sudden, I would find myself in a vortex of white noise…my heartbeat the only sound I could hear. Every other sound was just a muffled echo of the world outside of my head—the sounds made no sense. I could not think clearly, but for some unknown reason, I operated through it, and no one would have ever known what a crazy world I was living in at that moment.

One day in particular, something in my anxiety-filled life sparked a panic attack that was so physical I was sure I was having a heart attack. So, all by myself, husband in a combat zone, no family to call (I doubt I would have told them anyway), I packed my one-year- and three-year-old children up, with snacks, diapers, toys, and everything I needed to leave the house for a long while. I calmly (on the outside) put the kids in the car and drove to the emergency room twenty minutes away. Once I parked, I remember taking the stroller out of the trunk and opening it. Everything was all in slow motion. I see it all now as an old, silent black-and-white movie. I loaded up the stroller basket, then opened the door to get my one-year-old out and into the stroller. Then I got my three-year-old out of the car. I remember holding my daughter's hand as we walked across the parking lot and pushing the stroller into the emergency room entrance. Everything around me was happening in the slowest of motion, and in each second, I was still convinced I was having a heart attack.

I stood in line, still looking like a normal mom of two. I had become a master at hiding my panic attacks. To everyone around me, I looked like a relaxed and calm mother.

I got to the counter to get checked in and came face to face with a woman who looked at me with a big warm smile, thinking I was there for the kids. She asked what I needed, and I said in a whisper, "I think I am having a heart attack."

Looking back on this, I cannot believe I actually drove myself to the hospital thinking I was having a heart attack. The receptionist looked at me with a shocked look on her face, took my name, and sent me to the waiting room.

I went and sat in a jam-packed waiting room; hardly any chairs were available. The woman next to me complained that I would be there a long time because she had been there for hours already. Her voice sounded to me like an old tin can. Just then, the receptionist called my name. I could not have been there for more than five minutes. The complaining woman gave me a dirty look and groaned about me going through so quickly—some people were shaking their heads at me. They did not know what was happening in my mind, or that my world was utterly muffled, black and white, and I was operating in a strange vortex of fear. I felt nothing.... I was completely numb.

I got into a treatment room, and the nursing staff and a physician were treating me with some urgency. There I was, my one-year-old on the bed with me and my three-year-old in the stroller playing. While my son was on my chest, they were putting EKG stickers and wires on me. Again, all of this was happening while I was on another planet, in that very strange vortex. I have no idea how long I was in that treatment room. I have no idea what happened after that. Anxiety attacks tend to make time and the order of things get all mixed up. But I do remember a very kind doctor coming into the room, taking one look at my chart and my kids playing in the room, sitting down next to me, and saying, "Your heart is physically fine…. Are you under any stress?"

At that exact moment, I broke down into an utter release of sobs. The ugly cry was unleashed! (Poor doctor, I feel bad for him now; he was so kind.) But do you know, until that moment, I had never considered that I was under stress. I had never even thought about it. I had always looked at others' lives as much harder than mine. Many parents were doing more than me and dealing with worse situations. The majority of women I knew living in that area had husbands away at war, and they were also living their lives alone. The truth is many of us were living with similar types of anxiety, but none of us ever spoke about it.

The doctor tried to reassure me that stress was sometimes normal for military spouses and single parents. But I was not a single parent! Single parents have to do everything, from earning income to raising kids alone for the child's entire life. I would never equate what they do with my hardships. If anyone was allowed a panic attack, it was them. I did not. Both my sisters-in-law are single moms, and in my eyes, they are superheroes I admire more than they will ever know. Despite the doctor's reassurance that I was fine, very healthy, and not going to have a heart attack any time soon, I still had significant panic attacks…over and over again. Sometimes multiple times a day. I told no one.

I used to think if I died at home, no one would know I was gone, since I did not have core friends around me at that time and my family was all overseas. My kids, who were both still in cribs, would be stuck there for days before anyone knew I was gone. To ensure this would not happen, I asked a brand-new friend a few months later to call me every day at 7 a.m. to ensure I was alive. I am sure she thought I was insane, but she did it until the day my husband came home from Iraq, and it did actually relieve that particular parenting anxiety. This small gesture helped me more than she will ever know. Thinking about it now, I just laugh at how crazy the whole situation was and the craziness that sometimes surrounds us all as parents.

Let us be clear. Many parents at some stage (some parents at every stage) are struggling with something. Knowing this, let's remember to be calm, kind, and nonjudgmental with each other. We need to do this all the time. And if a mom or dad asks you for a little help, no matter how odd it might seem, please understand how vulnerable they are, how hard it is for them to ask for help, and how much they actually might need it. No matter how small or insignificant to you, it might be a huge deal to them under the stress of parenting.

With the help of family, speaking to friends, and a whole lot of self-actualization, I did eventually get my anxiety under control. Proper exercise, less sugar, and doing something fun every day helps me control myself. To me, fun is anything that makes you feel light again. Looking at the clouds, reading a book, taking a walk, gardening, cooking, running, painting, dancing, yoga, doing a puzzle, watching a movie, anything—it's all fun. Whatever makes you feel like your old self, brings joy to your life, or gives you a feeling of peace is fun. Take time every day to care for yourself. If you do not, "bad" emotions can build up before you know it.

**EXERCISES FOR WORKING WITH OVERWHELMING FEEL-INGS OR NEGATIVE THOUGHTS**

1.  What can you do daily to make you feel happy, ease your stress, and give you a sense of self? These activities do not have to take much time or energy, just give you a few moments of mindfulness and feeling like your old self.

    Write down the first five things that pop into your mind without overthinking.

    _____

    _____

    _____

    _____

    _____

2.  Positive affirmations—I have two sets of affirmations I use when I feel anxiety or negativity building up. I think of it as having a bucket that is filling up with negative thoughts, so I cram positive ones in until all the unpleasant ones have leaked out. I repeat these affirmations over and over until the negative feelings go away. If you think this might work for you, I recommend reading *You Can Heal Your Life* by Louise Hay.

    Think of four things you want to attract. Make them into a sentence happening in the now, and use the words "I am…" to begin. Do not use any negative words like *not, no, can't,* etc. Here are some I have recited for so many years that they feel like a part of me.

    I am confident.

I am successful.

I am a magnetic person.

I am successful in all I do.

Now it is your turn. Find those four things you would like to attract into your life. At first, they might not feel natural, but one day you might find yourself singing them in the shower or rocking to them in your car. Write them down here while you are thinking about it.

_____

_____

_____

_____

_____

3.  Labeling is a great tool to use and keep in your toolbox. Simply label the feelings or worries that come up. Let us say your mind gives you worry about being late. Just say to yourself "Late, the worry is being late." Then feel it melt away. If you are worried about a bill payment coming up, say, "Payment, the worry is the payment." Once you name the worry, it takes part of the power your mind has given it, and your worry, including the spiral to anxiety, can often burn out or slow down. Try it.

_____

_____

_____

_____

## TV TIME AND THEIR TECHNIQUES—for Younger Children

**Dora the Explorer**

I feel like every chapter should start with some disclaimer because I am by no means a perfect parent, whatever that means. The majority of lessons I've learned in all aspects of my life have been learned through significant failures. I figure if I can have a few mom wins a couple of times a week, I can claim colossal success. So, here is my confession: I have often used the TV as a nanny, and still do! And you know what…it's okay. As we spoke about earlier, sometimes we have to take time for ourselves, even to just stop and breathe. Sometimes—okay, it was daily—I used to sit and watch TV with the kids, maybe even close my eyes and get a twenty-minute rest after being up six times with a baby the night before. There, in those brain-dead moments, I suddenly realized we could all learn something from the sometimes-annoying kids' TV shows.

Take *Dora the Explorer*, for example. It became a big part of my life for a few torturous years. Kids will sit there thoroughly engaged for as long as we let them, and all because Dora starts by engaging them. She does that by having them remember four simple things in a row. Dora would say something like this:

> We are going to go…
> Through the fairy forest,
> Into the cave,
> Down the mountain,
> And around the road to Abuela's house.

Brilliant!

Through the fairy forest, into the cave, down the mountain, and then down the road to Abuela's house. Dora never has more than four things to remember.

I started implementing Dora's technique in our lives, and it changed everything. When I took the kids out in the morning, I said:

We are going to do four things today:

Go to the gym,
Then to the grocery store,
Then to friends,
Then home.

Gym,
Grocery store,
Friends,
Home.

Gym,
Grocery store,
Friends,
Home.

The children used to sing this over and over, just like Dora, knowing what was coming next. Dora's technique made it easier for them to understand what was going to happen in their normal days. Children have little to no concept of time; think about how long a normal day can be for them. Do you remember how long days were for you as a kid?

At the beginning of the week, most people look at their calendar to see what they have on it and then determine what needs to happen to get everything done. Then again, in the morning, some check to see what the day holds, just as a reminder. Now imagine how it feels to be a child going through day-to-day life not knowing what you are doing or where you are going in a very big and sometimes scary world. Adults feel more comfortable knowing what is going on, so why wouldn't children? They need to understand what is happening in the day. It makes them more comfortable in that big scary world, and they can also pace themselves because days never seem to end when you are a child.

When a child understands what their day entails, they are often more at ease. Less wondering. Fewer questions. More understanding. More comfort. Put another way, if we give kids clear markers for the day so they can focus on where they are in the long day, it makes daily life simpler and easier for them to understand. And simple for kids is always better. If you need them to be still and not run around, you can remind them of the next part of their day. Example. Post office, park, shop, home. When they are in the post office, they know the park is next, and that is where they can play. If they do not know what comes next, they will take any (and I mean any) opportunity to play, because that is what kids do and are intended to do: play.

A couple of weeks ago, I met with Liz, a friend and incredible mother who has a four-year-old. Liz helps other mothers all over the world with her business. When we met one morning, she looked worn and shared that the morning routine with her daughter was not pleasant; she wished it could be calm and happy instead of rushed and frustrated. When we are on timelines, parents tend to be a little bit more elevated, and the kids can feel that elevation. Liz was saying they do the same thing every day, but she still ends up nagging her child every day about the same things.

I mentioned the Dora technique, where she could put what she needs done in a Dora rhyme. Dress, eat, teeth, shoes…dress, eat, teeth, shoes. She agreed to give it a try. A couple of weeks after, I saw her again, and she came up to me immediately, and said, "I must thank you for the Dora technique. It worked!" My heart sang for her. What this actually meant was Liz and her child had a calm and happy morning instead of a rushed and frustrated one. Both the mother *and* the child benefitted…and all thanks to Dora, my in-the-moment babysitter.

### Thomas the Tank Engine

They're two, they're four, they're six, they're eight. Shunting trucks and hauling freight…you know, and now the song is stuck in your mind—you're welcome.

Shows like *Thomas and Friends*, about Thomas the Tank Engine, have messages you can bring into your home just like Dora does.

Thomas was a useful engine and every child who watches his shows knows this. So, let's use that with our children. How can we make our children feel useful just like Thomas? Can our kids be useful in the house? Can our children contribute in the home like the parents do? Even the smallest task can help in a busy household. Picking up toys. Putting dirty clothes in the hamper. Making the bed. Taking trash out. Whatever is age appropriate. Thomas demonstrates that everyone can be useful. We, as parents, can demonstrate that everyone in the family can be useful as well. More importantly, everyone who benefits from the family also has to assist the family.

A similar concept is shared by Julie Lythcott-Haims, who served as the dean of freshman and undergraduate advising for a decade at Stanford University. She is also the author of *How to Raise an Adult*. In her TED talk, Julie said, "Childhood provides a foundation for their success built on love and chores." Yes, she said chores. The earlier they begin, the better, too. What happens now (and I am a notorious culprit of this) is we do not give our kids enough or any chores because we want them to focus on other things like school, sports, etc. But what we are stripping from our children is, as Julie says, "the mindset of, there is work to do, it is unpleasant, but someone's got to do it, and it might as well be me." She adds that children should "contribute their efforts to the betterment of the whole." The study found that this mindset was the main ingredient in professional success. You can find Julie Lythcott-Haims on Ted Talks or by googling her. I highly recommend looking her up.

### Understanding Themselves—Inside Out

Along with Dora and Thomas, the *Inside Out* movie is a great tool. I only saw it as a tool after my daughter's school in Australia did a project on it to explore the children's emotions. If you have not seen it, be sure to have a watch. It is actually really good. The movie is from the point of view of the emotions of the lead character, which all live in a girl's mind. There is Joy, Anger, Disgust, Sadness, and Fear. It shows how they all work together and are all needed in a person's life. This movie can help parents talk with children about how they feel. It gives the child a visual place to start that they can understand. When your child is happy or sad, angry or even frustrated, you can speak to them about their feelings, and more importantly, what to do with those feelings and relate it to the movie plot. It is a simple and easy-to-understand way of discussing a complicated topic with your children.

I always thought they should add "mean girl" to the list of characters in the movie since many of us have one of those in our minds. I often told my daughter when she hit the tween years that she needed to control her inner mean girl because it was not kind to her. I would make her see the mean girl in her mind's eye and kick it out the door, shouting, "You are not welcome here!"

### Rules 123

Just like in the Dora game, children do better when they have less information and if it is repeated often. Our family uses this guideline whenever possible because it just makes life easier. We only have three rules at a time, and we adjust them depending on age. We recite these rules when going to shopping malls, amusement parks, zoos, city walks, wherever and whenever the family is in a busy area and a bit more control is needed.

During their young years, our rules were:

Rule 1 – Always listen to Mommy and Daddy
Rule 2 – Stay close
Rule 3 – Have fun

For older children it can be:

Rule 1 – Stay in the park
Rule 2 – Stay together
Rule 3 – Have fun

Rules 123 can be applied anywhere and under many situations. They just have to be simple and easy to remember. Deric used the Rules 123 method with his Little League teams. Each week, before practice, they would recite them back to him with enthusiasm.

Rule 1 – Do your best
Rule 2 – Be a good teammate
Rule 3 – Have fun

Most of the time, Rule 3 can be "have fun," so the first two rules should be essential to your family or the situation. But keeping Rule 3 as "have fun" reminds the kids that as long as they follow the first two rules, there is always room for a little fun. Eventually, you just need to say, "What are the three rules?" and they will spurt them out with enthusiasm, proud they remembered.

What can your Rules 123 be when you are out and about?

Rule 1 - _____

Rule 2 - _____

Rule 3 - _____

There you have it; my TV nanny was educational. Mom win!

**LESSONS LEARNED**

- Parents are not perfect.

- Everyone must rest, child and parent.

- Parenting is hard; it's harder when you are tired. Give yourself a break.

- Take time to relieve stress and build systems to help you along the way.

- Find your positive affirmations and use them.

- When a child understands their day, they are more at ease (The Dora Technique).

- Everyone in the home can be useful (The Thomas Technique).

- The sooner children start contributing, the better (for them and for you).

- The *Inside Out* movie is a great tool.

- A calm parent is a better parent. Find ways to stay calm.

CHAPTER 9

# PARENTING PRACTICES FROM THE UNITED STATES OF AMERICA

*"Immigration is the sincerest form of flattery."*

— Jack Paar

## COMING TO AMERICA

I have never been to a country as diverse as America. Each state, each city, is a melting pot in some way. It really is a country of immigrants; children can have a group of friends where none of them look alike. The diversity runs into every aspect of the country from politics to food options. No wonder there is a hub of excitement and energy wherever you go.

In 2005, I married my husband Deric and moved from London to the United States. Since we were moving to Fayetteville, North Carolina, from one of the oldest and largest cities in all of Europe, it was a huge change, to say the least. Now, any move to a new country comes with a move into a new culture, so it can be quite a shock to the system. It is hard to bypass that "shock on the system" phase. You actually need to go through it while you figure out your new reality. I laugh now at what made me feel uneasy or shocked when I first moved to the United States. One of those uneasy feelings was the enormous choice of absolutely everything. If you ever want to see a foreigner overwhelmed, send them to buy toilet paper or toothpaste from Walmart. The variations on one product are enough to send their minds spinning. Just going to the grocery store was something I had to brace myself for because there were so many options for everything. It would take me hours to get through the aisles and navigate my way through all the possibilities. I am explaining all this for good reason in a parenting book because I honestly think if you ever want to be reminded what it feels like to be a child, immigrate to another nation. (Or at least imagine it.) Everything is new. Everything is big. And everything is a choice you know little to nothing about. Just like it felt moving to the United States, but way worse.

Another uneasy feeling was eating out at restaurants. In Europe, when you go out to eat at a restaurant, you get a table for the night, and you calmly enjoy an evening of no cooking or cleaning up. Eating out is an event, one you dress for, and leave a massive gap in your calendar to enjoy. In the United States, it is a normal occurrence where you just grab a bite, literally. Then while you are eating, usually halfway through the meal, your bill is placed on the table by a pleasant server so you can pay and leave quickly. I was stunned in America when I was welcomed by happy, talkative staff and servers. They would ask about my day, where I was going afterward, what was in my shopping bags—the conversations were endless. If you have ever eaten in Europe, you will know this does not happen. You might get a grunt from a server some days, and that would be on a good day. To make things even worse for my poor shocked state, I was living in the South, which must be the friendliest, warmest, most welcoming place on the planet.

Small talk was another challenge for me to figure out. Most days, I was like a deer in headlights when everyone started a small, chit-chat conversation with me. I now, however, pride myself on my ability to speak to anyone, anywhere. Even the cashiers in our local grocery store became friendly, familiar faces. I even knew about their kids, their vacations, and I once bought a cashier a flower as a celebration for her new grandbaby she was advertising to everyone who came into her happy space. Eventually, these small moments with humans were what got me through some very uneasy times during my integration into what I soon learned was a truly extraordinary country.

A few years later, after finally starting to understand North Carolina and America's South, my husband and I moved to Kansas City with our twenty-month-old and a newborn. I was again apprehensive with the move and all its change, but I soon fell in love with America's Midwest. Since I had begun to master the chit chat and small talk, normal events soon became very personal encounters. Even going in to pay my electric bill, the ladies knew my children and me by name and always commented on how big the kids were getting. They knew and remembered our previous conversations and would speak about a subject that had happened a month prior. "Did you ever find someone to clean your gutters?" or "How was that new dentist you tried last month?" Friendship can be found anywhere in America. It was amazing to experience from an outsider's perspective.

After less than a year in Kansas, we were moved to Washington State, a place I still say I am from since I believe I could live the rest of my life there. The people were genuine and welcoming, loving to newcomers. I grew to love this community, and leaving three years later to move back to Europe almost broke my heart.

Luckily for us, a few years later, we found ourselves back in the United States, this time in Southern Virginia. Our first day there we had two meals on our doorstep. Somehow word got out that we were waiting for our furniture to arrive, so someone I had never met came over to drop off a blow-up mattress, bedding, and towels. Then, just a few days later, we were "officially" welcomed to the neighborhood at the community pool during a very humid Virginia Fourth of July celebration. Everywhere we went, we were welcomed. At my daughter's dance school and my son's Tai Kwon Do school, parents came up to me and asked if I was new to the area, welcomed us, and then asked if we needed anything. Our new home in Virginia felt like a familiar, loving village within the first few months. Each week, I had a home to drop in on for a tea, or a chat, usually just going through the back door because it was always open for anyone to drop in. When I felt like people and a conversation, all I needed to do was stand outside my house, and within minutes, someone was walking by and would stop for a chat.

When we lived in Europe, it was different. Not bad by any means—it was wonderful in many ways, just very different from America. Europeans would ask us about our journey around the world, probably because I have a South African accent, my husband is an all-American boy, and both my kids had full British accents at the time. We were a very unusual family for sure, and customs at the airport always took a bit of time. But no matter where I go in the world, whether it is Europe, Africa, or Australia, I am always asked the same questions by locals. "What is the best country you have ever lived in?" and "What do you think of our country?"

I can share with you now that I truly believe every country is fabulous! Every single one has something fantastic to fall in love with, but I will also share that there is no perfect place. The grass is not greener on the other side, and it will still need to be mowed. I won't go into all the good and bad we experienced in each place, but when we leave each country, we choose to take the good with us, and that is what I share here.

Another question I got in Europe often surprised me, and the first few times it was asked, I had no idea how to answer it. Now, however, I am happy it was asked because I have been able to consider it over the years. The question often asked was, "Does America have a culture?" It may seem a strange question from an American perspective, but to the rest of the world, the United States can be very confusing.

There are so many cultures in the United States, and it is such a large country. Many people around the world only know America from what Hollywood or news programs show them. I actually remember seeing my first yellow school bus in America and squealing like a child because I did not think they were real. I was shocked to find out they were used every day! I absolutely thought they were just in TV shows and Hollywood films. Not only that, but unless you have experienced the South, then gone to New York and California, it is hard to understand that every region in America, even state to state, is entirely different—like mini-countries in one gigantic country.

With all of these cultural differences and perspectives bouncing around my mind from every country I have lived in and visited, I found one common thread running through the United States—the North, South, East, West and everywhere in-between. That common thread was the culture of the United States. And America's culture is kindness. Simple kindness. Despite everything bad we see in the news and all the negativity surrounding the latest tragedy or all the political differences, I still stand behind this idea because I have never had so much kindness shown to me and my family as in the United States. Not just in one state, but in all the states we lived in and visited through-out our journey. If anyone in a community asks for help, the whole community turns out to help them. When kids have a lemonade stand on the corner, strangers stop their cars, grab a cookie and lemonade, and always over-pay. It is not uncommon to go through a Starbucks drive-thru to find out someone in front of you just bought your coffee; nor is it strange to help the mom who does not have enough money at the grocery store checkout line. This type of kindness happens on a global scale as well. When a country needs assistance or has a horrific natural disaster, America always seems to be the first one there to help and open its wallets. Every time.

Kindness is everywhere in the United States and sometimes in the most unusual places. When you stop and acknowledge the person smiling at you from across the store or politely respond to the person asking how your day is, this kindness is something you might take for granted when that is all you have ever known, or even get annoyed about because you have been asked the same question ten times that day. But, if kindness ever goes away, or you move to another country where this type of warm, welcoming hospitality and kindness is not the norm, and no one asks or even cares to connect or greet a stranger, that is when you feel the loss of it. That is when you can actually appreciate the kindness shown in the smallest of ways every day throughout the United States. I am so very lucky to have lived in so many countries around the world and experienced so many cultures so I can see America's kindness as something truly special.

## WORK LIKE A MOTHER

Like in most countries, American moms come in all flavors. In such a big country, it would never be fair to put everyone in one box or presume to know how everyone parents. Some states' parents are more competitive than others, while some are relaxed and let their kids be kids. I always found throughout the world a big divide between working and non-working moms. I have yet to see which one is the most accepted. When I was working, I would get the side comments about how I was not at home with my kids. When I was not working, I would get the side comments about how I did not do enough. I wondered where the sweet spot was, where I could dodge all the remarks. Or even if there is such a place.

In Southern Virginia, two incredible women came into my life, and I got to see two perfect, but opposite moms right under my nose: Melissa and Amy. Both opened my eyes to what it means to be a mother, and I learned so much from them, so of course, their stories absolutely need to be shared.

Melissa is a high-powered CEO of her own company. She is driven, stylish (so stylish), a PTA president, has three great kids, and a wonderful husband. Basically, the whole package. She is the all-American working mom, balancing life, business, and family as best she can. She was my voice of reason, the person I would bring my problems to. Melissa got me out and about when I was in a funk, and she made me look at situations from many angles, keeping me on track. She is the perfect friend everyone needs. Melissa's internal drive was to help people. She poured love into her community; even when she did not feel like it or had a dozen other things going on, she was always there for everyone.

Amy was a stay-at-home mom. Her focus was her family, her home, and all the thousand things stay-at-home moms do that no one sees. Amy was one of the most relaxed people I have ever met. She brought people together and made us laugh more than anyone has made me laugh in years. She brought so much happiness to not only her wonderful husband and children, but to everyone she came into contact with throughout her day. It was her super power. Amy described herself perfectly as a twelve-year-old boy in a forty-two-year-old woman's body, and I could not explain her better. She was the girl everyone wanted as their friend. I was so happy she was mine. Amy taught me that even though we need to adult, even though we have a tremendously important job as a mother and have so many associated responsibilities, it is okay to stay young at heart and have some fun while you do it.

So, as you might be able to imagine, Amy, Melissa, and I were tight—take a bullet for each other tight. I unconditionally love their children like they are blood and still consider them both family. This closeness allowed me to see both sides of the mom coin. During my time living in the same neighborhood as Amy and Melissa, I was teaching ten to twelve hours a week, hardly a full-time job, plus some volunteering and running my home business. For the first time, I was in the middle, right in between a working mom and a stay-at-home mom, and right in between Amy and Melissa. The interesting part was, from the center, I could see more clearly. And what I saw made me realize something very important. Both families were perfect. They had both found a life that was right for their specific needs and their individual choice either to work or stay at home made them better as women and happier as a families.

We all have different family needs and wants. What a family chooses is all about them; they know what works for them and what does not—no one else does. If Melissa had been a stay-at-home mom, she would have been miserable, and if Amy had decided to open a business, she would have been miserable. The funny saying, "If a mom ain't happy, then no one is!" is very accurate. My point? Not all women are meant to be working moms, and not all women are meant to be stay-at-home moms. Do what is right for your family; do what is right for you. Then go hang out with all the people doing it differently and be in awe of them and how fabulous they are.

And for all those dads out there, that goes for you too.

## ONE WOMAN'S GIFT TO ALL WOMEN

Seldom do you get perfect neighbors, but when you do, you hold on to them so tightly and make sure they do not leave. My family had this experience when living in Germany. Our house had a shared garden (well, no fence between and no one cared where the line was). Our neighbors were Allison and Tim and their three fun and fabulous children, a family that was calm, had no stress, and best of all, was positive. I have to confess, when I met them, I needed the lessons they had to share. I was becoming rigid and set in my ways, trying so hard to be a consistent parent and tick off all the boxes we are "meant" to tick. And then, a lesson I truly needed (and my family needed) was placed a few feet away from me.

Allison is the most put-together person; she always gets things done, but always in her own time. Her famous saying is, "Leave it to the last minute, and it will only take a minute." During our time as neighbors, we both had military work events at our homes. I would prep for weeks and set the house up for dozens of guests days ahead. Allison, on the other hand, would not stress at all, and it was common for her to still be sitting at my house having a cocktail in the kitchen an hour before everyone was due to arrive at her house. This family was without a doubt the calmest, no-fuss group of people we had ever met, and we loved them for it.

Allison taught me a ton of things about chilling out and trusting everything will be just fine, but one thing she taught me I must share.

Usually, when I hear someone is coming over to my house, I do a quick sweep and clean up as much as I can as quickly as I can. I would clean the kitchen, fill the dishwasher, clean the guest bathroom, hide the laundry in a wardrobe (note: hide and not do), then open the door to let whomever was coming think this is my normal.

At Allison's house, it was different. People dropped in for a quick chat and a visit every day. When I arrived (usually by letting myself in through the back door), it was normal to find her sitting with someone in her lounge. I would arrive to an always clean house, but usually not perfect, and some days were worse than others. Laundry she was going to get to soon was often on the couch, and there would always be shoes lying around she was going to get to putting away. She would say, "Hello. Just throw that laundry on the table and sit." The best part of her being more focused on the people in her home than the home itself was when she came to visit me, I could do the same thing. I would let her in without doing my normal guest clean-up, and it was so relieving. Allison gave every woman who walked through her door the gift of not always having everything in order, and not having a perfect, put-together house. When all those women sat in her home, they were welcomed with no expectation to be perfect.

Allison gave every parent the gift of chilling out and just being whoever you are on that day. No need for fancy clothes, makeup, or airs
and graces. Our true, honest selves were always welcome and completely accepted. Quality time with her kids and family was her priority every single day. She taught me, and all the moms who used to
rotate through her door, that a perfect house and a fake-looking life
mean absolutely nothing. It was the connections, the people, and the
conversations that made her life full, not a perfect house.

## OPRAH

I think Oprah Winfrey is an American treasure. I loved her even
before I came to the United States. Before her daily talk show ended,
I used to make sure the kids and I were home at 4 p.m. daily so I
could start dinner and watch Oprah while cooking. It was my most
special time of the day. To the kids, I used to call this time "Kailey
and Devin time," meaning everyone had to play on their own and
by themselves. This time was created for two reasons. One was so
I could watch Oprah without interruptions, which was incredibly
important for my sanity at the time. The second reason was so each
child did not get used to someone always entertaining them and they
could become comfortable playing by themselves. I did this in the
hopes that in the future, each child would be more than comfortable
with their own company and would rarely need anyone to fill their
time and entertain them. There are so many times and things we
do as adults that require us to be alone, and unfortunately, many
adults struggle with this. Eating a meal at a restaurant alone, attend-
ing events alone, working alone, or traveling alone is seldom seen.
Sometimes we have to function in life independently and without
assistance as teenagers and then as adults. So daily, during Oprah, I
provided a time for the kids to develop their self-reliance skills. If a
child can develop comfort in their own personal time, it will surely
be a gift of freedom in their future.

During one of my Oprah days, Oprah was interviewing the magnificent Maya Angelou. I do not even think I cooked that day; I just sat and listened to this incredible woman speak. She shared something about parenting I will never forget, and some days, I find myself holding my tongue because of her advice that day.

Maya Angelou was asked about parenting and growing strong children. She explained to Oprah that how you physically look at your children (your facial expressions) and how you welcome your child is how the child will look at themselves. The way a parent speaks to a child will become that child's inner voice. If your child walks into a room and they look like a mess, say nothing. Greet them first with love and speak to them kindly; later deal with the mess. If your child asks a not-so-smart question, just smile and answer it. If you always criticize a child, they will always find fault with themselves and think they are not enough. This is not what we want for our future child, so it is up to us to help ensure it does not happen.

Maya Angelou said it is easy in the moment of a busy life to jump on our children for their messy hair or their outfit not matching, but wait! Take a breath and see if it is the right time for this correction or lesson because it might not be. The worst thing that will happen is they will look like a mess, and to be honest, you are the only one who cares anyway.

**GREAT EXPECTATIONS**

The best part of becoming a parent is everyone will give you an opinion on your child. And the worst part about parenting is that everyone will give you an opinion on your child. Even as I say that, I am 100 percent sure I have given my opinion to some poor, unsuspecting mom who thought, *Really?* To all those moms, I apologize. We have all done it, and will continue to do so because that is how we operate. Most people are honestly just trying to help. But not everything is helpful.

One morning at the doctor's office, I was getting my flu shot. I happened to have a nurse who was pregnant, so we got to chatting about the baby, and she told me she had a two-year-old at home, too. She became quite sad as she said, "I am trying to enjoy this time because any day now, she will start to hate me." Wait...what? I could not leave the office until she understood that did not have to be true. She said she has heard from other moms that all kids eventually start to hate their parents. I was dumbfounded. Is that what we as parents are sharing? No! I refuse to believe it has to be that way.

Another time, I met a woman from my local gym class. She was a bubbly, happy mom of three, and I was immediately drawn to her. We would chat after class each week. One day she asked me how old my children were, and when I told her they were seven and nine, she said, "Oh, they are still sweet." *What? Why can't they always be sweet and kind?* I thought to myself.

I went looking around for moms whose children were grown to ask their opinion on this very upsetting topic.

In Norfolk, Virginia, I ended up sharing a table at a restaurant with a woman. We were both grabbing lunches during the busy time of the day at a restaurant where no tables were available. She came over and gently asked if she could share the table. I happily agreed. In true American style, sharing the table did not just mean sharing the space, but also the time. Her name was Kate, and she worked in the area. Kate had three teenagers, and one was heading off to college. (It is amazing how much you can learn about a person over a quick lunch in America!) I point blank asked her if her kids were terrible, awful, monstrous teenagers. She looked at me like she was going to burst out laughing. I stared at her with a straight face, completely serious. "Oh," she said, "you are serious. Honey, who have you been talking to?"

"Many people," I replied. "Apparently, I only have two good years left before my oldest is thirteen and then turns on me and hates me."

Kate laughed. "Sweetie," she said in her wonderful Southern accent, "it is all about communication." She went on to explain that the more you speak with your children, the more they will understand that they will have strong feelings they will want to take out on you. Parents and siblings are easy targets. If they act out with a friend, they run the risk of the friendship ending, and no child wants that. But a parent will never leave them, so they get to act out against them and know their mother, father, or sibling will never leave them.

Kate gave me time to let this sink in; then she explained that she lets her tweens and teens know they might have the need to yell or say mean things, but in no way is that okay. Her children knew from an early age that angry, hateful feelings were, much of the time, just hormone changes or feelings they did not yet understand. When her children started feeling angry and ready to explode on someone, they would come to their parents and simply tell them that feelings were building up. I asked Kate what she did with that information. She said, "I made them go run around outside."

I have since shared Kate's conversation and ideas with my kids. I explained how they might feel super-angry and hate-filled one day, and that they will want to lash out at me or Dad because we are the easy targets. But they could not. We were the people they should respect and love the most. Parents and siblings have been the ones who have loved them since the day they were born. Just because we will never leave them does not mean they get to unleash horrible feelings on us when something is going wrong. As Kate told me, "It's all about communication." We have to keep our parent-child communication lines open. We need to remind our children from a very early age that feelings are normal—good feelings and bad feelings. But lashing out when bad feelings come up is not acceptable. If we provide this lesson to our children early, when those tantrums start to show their ugly heads, we have a good chance of preventing this stereotypical "kids hating their parents" phase before it even begins. It has worked for me most of the time, but when it does not, I send my kids to run around the garden.

## LET'S TALK ABOUT SEX, BABY

Yes…we are going to talk about sex, but first, we are going to talk about periods. And it is okay. They happen all the time. Monthly, in fact, to every woman you know and every single woman on the planet.

When we were in the United States, the time for the talk with my daughter about sex and body changes arrived. It is the conversation all parents dread. Our angelic babies, who one moment are convinced unicorns are real, then start asking complicated questions. And they feel our anxiety when we don't know what to say. As usual, I reached out to my mom gurus around the world for help. My friend Samantha was the perfect choice. She was a good friend with four children who also was my yoga teacher. Her relationship with her kids and their respect for each other has always intrigued me. She is a big advocate for positive and open communication with her children. So open, in fact, that she was 100 percent comfortable speaking to her children about her monthly periods.

Samantha would call her periods her moon cycles so they could be seen as entirely natural and connected to the earth, not some strange "curse" like many of us are brought up to believe. She taught me that if possible, on the first day of your "moon cycle," you should take a rest, do either light exercise or no exercise, and give yourself some time, pampering yourself or just being still. I have done this since she told me about it, and now, the first day of my cycle is a day I look forward to instead of complaining about it or dreading it. I now see it as a day for cake, or something indulgent I don't often allow myself. The best is when I have a free day, and I am able to unplug and allow my body to rest. This is not always possible, but it certainly is a great feeling to yell in front of your kids, "Yay! I get a day off," or "Yay! I get to have cake today." My daughter sees it, and hopefully, over her years of many periods, she too will see it as a celebration day, not a dreaded day to complain about. It is simply a matter of how you look at it. Just the other day, Kailey came home from school and said, "Mom, it's ice-cream time," with a massive smile on her face. I was thrilled this was the attitude she would start with for the future 400-plus periods she will experience over her lifetime.

The actual sex talk began over drinks at home in Suffolk, Virginia, with our dear friend Jonathan, a doctor who not only was a man of deep faith, but also had a love of science. His daughter was ten—a year older than my daughter Kailey. He whispered to us that they had just had "the talk" with her. Flabbergasted, I felt like I had just been struck with a pan in my face. Was it that time already? Knowing before he spoke that whatever he told her would have been both caring and informative, Deric and I grilled him about what he said.

Jonathan told us he and his wife made the point to have the talk together, so as a dad, he could also be in a place where she could ask him questions too. He said he spoke purely from a medical and physical perspective, saying that humans were mammals and sex was utterly natural. They also emphasized self-respect and love. That was it. Nature. Science. Respect. Love. Done.

All those years of stressing were crushed in a few short minutes. I was so annoyed that I had stressed about this conversation for so many years. What a waste of worry. Now the sex talk seemed so simple to me. It would be normal, factual, with some talk about self-respect, love, and your faith sprinkled in. Easy. We pretty much followed precisely what Jonathan told us with our two children and made "the talk" so completely normal that the conversation was not weird at all. Nature. Science. Respect. Love. Done. Now, what would you like to have for dinner?

Knowing what fellow parents are saying and when they are saying it in your community helps you navigate the timing of the talk a bit as well. Knowing what a family whom we spent so much time with had just told their kids made the talk a more straightforward process, and when the kids compared notes, and they did, the notes were the same.

All you have to do is repeat this process, regularly, over the next several years.

That is right—the sex talk is not a one-and-done talk. We should have several talks about sex throughout our children's lives, and make each talk age-appropriate. Remember those open lines of communications? The sex talk is one of those lines of communication. Frank and honest discussions help everyone see sex as a normal part of life and make the topic more comfortable for children and parents. This open communication helps when really difficult sex topics come up, like STDs, pregnancy, sexual assault, etc. Everyone will be ready and comfortable enough to share and discuss these sometimes difficult topics.

To help keep difficult conversations age-appropriate (from questions about Santa to the sex talk), only answer the questions your children ask. No more. If they ask about A, answer only about A. When they are ready to hear B, they will ask about it, and so on. The trick is to be so open with them that they know they can ask anything, and you will always answer them without making them feel awkward. The moment they feel uncomfortable with you and with asking you questions is the moment they will go to their friends for answers, and who knows what information they are getting there—or worse, they google it and get bombarded with everything the internet can show them. So, keep them (and you) comfortable by answering only what they want to know. They will be back with more questions before you know it.

A great example of creating a normal, and in this case, funny environment to talk about sex comes from a neighbor and great friend from Germany. She took her thirteen-year-old son for lunch, and at the table said to him, "Let's just get something out the way. Say sex three times to my face, and then we can be done with the firsts." He did, and then burst out laughing. I love how she put the awkwardness on the table and got it out of the way. They both immediately became comfortable and were able to discuss the topic a bit more freely. Well done, Mom!

## MY G.I. JOE

My husband Deric has been in the Army for twenty-four years and has loved every year of it. This, of course, means that he has taken on a very disciplined, strong persona. How we ever ended up together, I will never know—we could not be more different, but opposites do attract. It was pure chance when we met outside a London club at 9:30 p.m. If I had joined the line one minute later, or if he had not asked me if the club was worth the wait, and if we had not both decided to stand in that line for two hours (drinking champagne on the sidewalk), I would never have known this life or had these stories to share.

But with an Army husband, some "military quirks" can seep into the home. Allow me to share what pops up in our house.

The military is leadership. It is what they work on and develop from the day a young man or woman raises their right hand and swears an oath to defend the Constitution of the United States. And since everything in the military is in bullet point format, I will try to explain my military lessons with the efficiency of military spouse training.

These are the terms my husband uses in our home regularly. At first, I rolled my eyes. Okay, I still roll my eyes. But as my kids grew, I started to see the method in his madness. Our children started to understand complex ideas like standards, risks, and values.

☐ **Risk mitigation:** The most dangerous time for a young adult is sixteen to twenty-two. Deric began "risk mitigation training" early in our children's lives, around five years old, and it was a direct pull from the risk mitigation concept he used daily in the Army. He tells the kids regularly that they are responsible for their own safety because he will not always be there to protect them. They must always look around and assess the risk to themselves and their friends, then mitigate that risk so no one gets hurt. He would give them age-specific examples year after year.

### 3-7 years old

o Hold Daddy's hand in the store so you don't get lost.
- Risk = Getting lost.
- Mitigation = Holding hands.

o Look both ways before crossing the street.
- Risk = Getting hit by a car.
- Mitigation = Looking both ways before crossing the street.

o Always wear a helmet on a bike/rollerblades.
- Risk = head trauma caused by a hard fall.
- Mitigation = wearing a helmet to prevent injury.

### 8-12 years old

o Don't throw the ball in the house next to the glass cabinet.
- Risk = Breaking glass cabinet and getting in massive trouble.
- Mitigation = Not throwing the ball near it.

o Be aware of your surroundings.
- Risk = Abduction.
- Mitigation = Staying clear of adult strangers in the local park.
- Risk = Getting hit by a car.

- Mitigation = Paying attention when moving through a parking lot.

## 12 and older

o Slow down! (roller blades, bike, car)
  - Risk = Crashing and getting hurt.
  - Mitigation = Slow down.

o Call/text when you get there.
  - Risk = Accidents and other emergencies
  - Mitigation = Knowing where the entire family is at all times.

    When life's risks are explained and seen in this manner, they can be more easily understood and assessed by children and then young adults (when it really matters). No matter what the situation, if children learn to first assess risk and then mitigate that risk with certain actions, they will be less likely to put themselves in high-risk situations, and if they do get in a tough spot, get themselves out safely.

Take a moment to think about three opportunities that are applicable to your family where you would like to teach your children about risk and mitigation.

1. Risk = _____

   Mitigation = _____

2. Risk = _____

   Mitigation = _____

3. Risk = _____

   Mitigation = _____

☐ **Values:** The military is a values-based organization and the US Army's values are an important part of Deric's life. The values are: Loyalty, Duty, Respect, Selfless Service, Honor, Integrity, and Personal Courage. (I think I have been positively brainwashed!) It was only natural, then, that our family would develop our own values. This was, of course, odd the first time I thought about it, but over the years, the Holbrook values became critically important to building our children's inner strength. Deric and I decided our values would be: be kind, strong, and smart. Each is easily understood by children and easily adaptable to any situation. Kind, strong, and smart is what we stand for and what we expect.

   o   Be Kind to everyone in every situation.
   o   Be Strong physically, mentally, spiritually, and physiologically.
   o   Be Smart: Book smart. Street smart. Make smart decisions.

Deric repeats these values regularly to the kids and brings them up when one of them is not kind, not strong, or not smart. He will immediately remind the kids what they are supposed to be and gently remind them what those words mean in our family. The kids know what their values are, and what we expect of them. It is truly amazing how well it works.

What do you think your family values are? Take some time to write them down here while you are thinking about it. It might take a conversation or two; they don't develop overnight. But knowing your family's values can set the stage for good behavior and a strong sense of self in your children at the earliest ages.

_____

_____

_____

_____

_____

_____

_____

_____

☐ **Standards:** In the military, standards are very important. So, of course, some military-type standards have creeped into our life. Do not get me wrong; our home is not an orderly place. Even though my husband would love to live in a museum, he, unfortunately, married me, who has 100 projects out all at once. (I will get to them all one day.) But we have standards and our children know them. That is the important part.

o   I expect the kids to offer everyone a drink when they get one for themselves.

o   I expect, if they are making food, that they offer some to everyone.

o   I expect that they will not shout in the car.

o   I expect that they will put their dirty clothes in the hamper.

o   I expect that they will keep their rooms relatively tidy.

What is a tidy room? What is the standard? You will often hear my kids say, "So, do I need to clean it to the 100 percent?" They know the standard from the very beginning of any situation. I often say, "Just make it 50 percent, and then we will go do something fun." But they both know what 100 percent is, and that's what matters to me.

What are the standards and expectations in your home? What are the expectations in a shop or restaurant? Take some time to write down your standards here. Then, of course, be sure to speak to your children about them using those open lines of communication.

What are your family's standards?

_____

_____

_____

_____

_____

_____

_____

## YOU ONLY CONTROL TWO THINGS

Just a few months ago, Deric and I met up with our friend Frank in Hawaii. Frank and Deric were fraternity brothers at the University of Hawaii. Frank was in the Marines and now works in the defense industry. He has two teenagers who are excelling in high school. I mean really excelling, like full-ride scholarships to private schools and college excelling. My husband took a page from my book and asked Frank what he did to get his children to this point. Frank, being a very smart husband, first gave his wife all the credit, and then explained that he reminds the children regularly what he learned in the Marines. You only have control of two things: your attitude and effort. Most other things are out of your and your children's control. But with the right attitude and right amount of effort, people can excel at anything they set their minds to.

Since then, every day, when the kids go to school, Deric yells out the door, "What can you control today?" They roll their eyes at him and reply, "Our attitude and effort, Dad." Positive brainwashing at its best.

## WORK-LIFE BALANCE

I wanted to end this military section with a story from a four-star general. My husband and I were invited to a talk with several hundred other Army families a few years back at a post in Kansas. This senior officer—who had spent nearly forty years in the Army, had lived all over the world, and had a very successful career—spoke very openly about the current state of the Army and the nation. At the end of his speech, he opened the floor to questions. I do not remember what he spoke about during the main portion of his speech, but I remember how he made me feel—like he was a man of substance. A spouse stood up in the auditorium, took the microphone, and asked him a very hard question: "What is the one thing you regret most about your military career?"

He paused as he contemplated how to answer. He then said, "I have had an extremely successful military career…but I have no relationship with my family."

The entire auditorium filled with stunned officers and their spouses was still. This great leader used this opportunity to warn the young officers (all in their mid-thirties and in the prime of their careers) about the importance of family over career. The room remained dead silent as he spoke deliberately and emotionally about finding a work-life balance. Sacrificing family for another promotion or a key assignment that might advance your career ultimately just takes you farther away from what is truly important. Family.

## LESSONS LEARNED

- As a child, everything is new, everything is big, and everything is a choice they know little to nothing about (see "Coming to America").

- America's culture is kindness.

- A family knows what works for them and what does not (see "Work Like a Mother").

- Not all women are meant to be working moms, and not all women are meant to be stay-at-home moms.

- Do what is right for your family. Do what is right for you.

- If a child is comfortable in their own personal time, it will surely be a gift of freedom in their future (see "Oprah").

- Take a breath and decide if it is the right time for this correction or lesson, because it might not be (see Maya Angelou's advice in "Oprah").

- It is all about communication (see Kate's advice in "Great Expectations").

- Feelings are normal. Lashing out, however, is unacceptable.

- Nature. Science. Respect. Love. Done. (see "Let's Talk About Sex, Baby")

- The sex talk is not a one-and-done talk.

- Only answer what your children ask. No more.

- You control only two things: your attitude and your effort.

- Develop your family values.

- Ensure family standards are known.

- Maintain a work-life balance that prioritizes family first.

# CHAPTER 10

# LEADING AND LEARNING BY EXAMPLE

*"Instruction is good for a child, but example is worth more."*

— *Alexandre Dumas*

## THE TANTRUM COOKIE

I love sharing! It hurts my heart when I see people at any age who are unable to share. Unfortunately, we see it all the time: Children unwilling to share a seat, toy, book, pencil, money, drink, food, etc. Showing children how to share is a gift that will last their lives and could actually end up helping hundreds of thousands of people. The ability to let go of physical items (stuff) will also help our children well into their adult years. Without attachment to physical items, there is less worry when those things ultimately get lost, destroyed, stolen, or simply break. When children see at a very early age that nothing actually happens when another child plays with their toys, or touches "their" things, or their favorite toy breaks, it is truly freeing, for both the child and the parent.

A very funny and memorable family lesson about sharing took place in a Panera Bread (a wonderful American bakery/coffee shop chain.)

Devin was two, and Kailey was four. Since I was a mother of two young children, I was operating on little sleep and needed coffee to make it through a normal day. I decided to go to Panera Bread for coffee and to get the kids a giant Panera cookie. When I asked Kailey and Devin if they wanted one of the massive M&M cookies, they both looked at me with so much excitement that I could tell the answer was yes. I collected my coffee and one large cookie from the counter, and then found a table in the packed seating area. After sitting everyone down, I took the *one* cookie I bought off its plate, broke it in half, and gave each of my children half. Immediately, Devin's face dropped. *What are you doing to my cookie?* he must have been thinking. He thought he and his sister would each get a whole cookie. Seeing the half M&M cookie on his plate, which, by the way, was his favorite type of cookie, my son decided to throw a tantrum—a performance deserving of an Oscar. In the packed Panera Bread store, Devin threw the salt and pepper shakers, the sugar packets, and everything on the table, demanding a full cookie. Everyone in the restaurant was looking at me, shocked and disgusted. (Or at least, that is what it felt like to me. They really just heard a commotion and looked over—a natural reaction.)

I showed no emotion at all to my Oscar-winning-tantrum child. I was as cold as ice, like nothing he could scream or throw could touch me. He had no power over me. Staring Devin straight in his eyes, I slowly reached over and took his half of the cookie off his plate. I stood up and slowly walked over to the trash can, making sure Devin could see where I was going. Still staring my son deep in his now tearing eyes, I held the cookie just above the trash can opening, released my grip, and let it fall straight into the trash. Then, calmly, with a little smirk on my face, I walked back to the table.

Devin was in shock. I could see the anger building in him even more, and his tantrum grew in intensity. I looked around the restaurant, and saw that an older couple were clapping for me and smiling away.

The older wife even gave me a thumbs up! (Their small indication of approval was such a huge deal to me. They will never know how much I needed it.) I told the kids we were leaving. My daughter grabbed her half of the cookie from the table and walked very politely next to me, trying to win the favorite child award, while I dragged my son, still crying, out of the restaurant and to the car. Still, with no emotion from me at all, I firmly put Devin into his car seat (you know when a mom gets her knees involved in getting a kid in a car seat, she is mad) and then settled my daughter into her car seat. We drove home, and I did not say one word to either child in the car. My daughter sat in the car quietly, still eating her half of the cookie; in the rearview mirror, I could see her looking over at her brother and smiling between bites. At this point, Devin lost his mind, screaming, kicking, and raging.

Once we got home, I got the kids out of the car and into the house. Then I laid down the rules. In the firmest manner I could, and with all my attention, I told Devin he would never act that way again and we would always share everything. Period. It was a harsh come-to-Jesus kind of moment, and I made sure, even at the age of two, it was one he would never forget.

That was the trick: Make the parenting lessons memorable. Extremely unpleasant (if required) but memorable for sure. Take things away, special things (like cookies), early bed, whatever nonviolent, non-physical "awakening" you can do to let the kids think, *Well, that sucked! I'm never going to do that again.* I know this works because, for years after that one very memorable, very emotional lesson, whenever my son got a cookie, any cookie, he immediately broke it in half, and looked for someone to share it with.

Even after the tantrum cookie incident, I consistently reminded my children, "When you share, you get more. If you share your things with someone, they will share theirs with you, and then you will have more." I said this so many times, they eventually started reciting it to friends when they were trying to share. I found the best way to explain this concept to children was like this: "If I have chips and you have cookies, I give you some chips, you give me some cookies, and immediately, you get more…you just had cookies, but now you have chips *and* cookies. It is the same with siblings' toys, food, games, and everything in between." This sharing concept does take time and consistency to teach, but it actually serves two purposes. It teaches sharing and reduces a child's (and hopefully an adult's) attachment to "things." In a world where we are advertised to and sold to everywhere from an early age, a little bit of detachment from "things" and a whole lot of sharing would probably do us all some good. This idea was shown to me in college by my friend Lara and her mother and sister. Whenever they ate, they shared everything, and they would naturally eat off each other's plates with no issues. I remember thinking "They are getting so much more than just what they ordered."

To help ensure these sharing values are upheld all year long, we adopted a rule from my magnificent friend Jenn's family in the United States. I loved it so much that we included it as part of our family sharing values. During Christmas, and birthdays for that matter, when you get a present, it belongs to you for forty-eight hours. After that, it belongs to the house…and everyone can use it. Bam! Done! No more my toy this or my toy that. The rule is every toy belongs to the house and not to any particular child. It is immediately a share toy. Now this might cause some angst in the very beginning, but over the long term, this simple sharing lesson will save so many problems. Although both kids have toys they prefer and they respect each other's preferences, this concept takes away all emotional connection to a "thing" that then becomes negative. The real lesson is their understanding they lose nothing by sharing. I've seen children get so emotional when sharing that they land up living in a "mine" world. This concept opens up more flow in a child's life and less attachment to what they own. When there is an issue and both or multiple children want to play with the same toy at the same time, it forces them to have to share and that is the lesson.

## THE GIFT OF VOLUNTEERING

Do you know anyone who volunteers? What do their lives look like to you? Are they happy? I will bet the answer is yes.

Tony Robbins said, "If you feel depressed and live too much in your head, get out and help someone else." I have found this to be true over the years. Every time I volunteer, my life improves exponentially, and so does my state of mind. Whether you help out at church, school, or in an organization that lights you up, it really could have a positive effect on you and your family.

My mother used to volunteer for disaster relief at the South African Red Cross. She would take my brother and me into community halls to sort donated clothes and household goods. These goods would then be distributed to families in Lesotho or throughout South Africa who lost their homes due to floods, fires, or other disasters. It was a massive eye-opener as a child to watch hundreds of people giving up their time and energy to help others they had never met and would never meet.

When I was growing up, my neighbor Anne showed me that volunteering could be a powerful addition to the community. Anne used to volunteer at the local Down syndrome school and would take me along to help out. She would make the loveliest items and trinkets to sell at the school fetes (fairs) for weeks before each event. I would run over to her house after school to help her stuff candy in toilet paper rolls, then wrap them like Christmas crackers. It lit me up on the inside like nothing else.

When you give freely, without expectations, your children see it, and something magical happens, kind of like sharing as a child. (When you share you get more!)

Deric has volunteered as a Little League coach for the past six years. I can see how much each and every baseball team means to him. The players can see it as well, especially Devin. When you offer your talent for no money, you will notice how much more you give and will feel so much better for it as well.

An amazing volunteer I have met is Tiffany, the creator of the One27 Initiative (one27initiative.org). She lives in Virginia and supports foster care programs around the state. Her organization provides bags and backpacks filled with age-appropriate pajamas, clothes, toiletries, and toys. The bags are for foster kids to take when they are removed from home, so they do not have to put their belongings in a garbage bag like many children in this unfortunate situation often do. The bags can provide just a little bit of comfort and ownership during an incredibly difficult time for these children.

Not all of us need to do big things like Tiffany, but opening our children's eyes to the power of helping others and the simple act of sharing is important and rewarding. If you give, you receive at the same time. It feels like you are a part of something bigger than yourself, and it brings humanity into your home and the children's developmental process. If we all do what we can to teach our children to think of others each day, it would not only benefit them, but make a meaningful change in our communities, wherever we may be in the world.

I am so grateful to all the people who have taught me the gift of volunteering. Let's take some time now to think about opportunities to volunteer.

Where could you volunteer to demonstrate both the power of giving and helping to your children *and* to help your community?

_____

_____

_____

_____

_____

## MILITARY SPOUSES AND VOLUNTEERING

I am drawn to those who give their time, energy, and love freely; that is why I feel so blessed to be a military spouse. The military spouse community helps others with no questions asked. They do not even need to know or like you, but they will show up when asked. Maybe that is why I am so proud to be called a military spouse. All around you, people are serving in some capacity, no matter how small, to help others. It is truly an incredible example for children to see and experience.

A perfect example of the spirit of the military spouse community and the power of giving happened a few years ago when our community, and the world itself, lost a beautiful soul. Her name was Ivey. Ivey was an FRG (Family Readiness Group) leader for Deric's unit. Being an FRG leader is a hard job. It is filled by a spouse volunteer and focuses on the betterment of families in military units. Ivey planned events and activities to bring families together during often extremely stressful combat deployments. She looked after dozens, if not hundreds of families, and went above and beyond for every person she met. During the time Ivey was our unit's FRG leader, she was diagnosed with aggressive breast cancer. She was also pregnant at the time. Our hearts broke. But what happened next changed how I perceive volunteering and how I understand what really happens when people come together to support one another.

With two children in school and her husband at work every day, and the weight of life on her shoulders, Ivey was overwhelmed by the cancer treatments and constantly felt ill. Word got out among the FRG. About twenty people showed up to help. All the volunteers were put on rosters, and everyone had a role. Some collected her children from school; others helped them with homework. Others did her grocery shopping. One woman took charge of Ivey's personal needs when she could not physically manage herself. I was part of the group that cooked for the family. Our cooking group delivered a few dinners every week to yet another volunteer, who would then deliver the meals to Ivey daily. This system helped limit the number and variety of germs that got into the home. Our military spouse volunteers did this for two years, showing the consistency, effort, and love of the community. Ivey was a blessing to us all, and each and every volunteer gave freely. We all learned so much from the experience, and I hope Ivey felt loved and cared for during those hard years of her far-too-short life.

## BOOKS THAT COULD CHANGE YOUR LIFE

Sometimes a book comes along and changes your life. I have come across a few so far, and I always, always share them. (Because when you share, you get more!) Now, it is time to share these two influential books—*The Four Agreements* and *The Five Love Languages*—with you. Each of these books helped me with my family, provided countless lessons along the way, and helped teach me how to truly lead by example. These are not parenting "how to" books, but books that actually teach complex life lessons we can apply to parenting.

### *The Four Agreements*

*The Four Agreements* is a very popular book by Don Miguel Ruiz published in 1997. My friend Tish bought it for me as a gift, saying, "You have to read this." And I did…ten times. I even have the agreements posted on my fridge. It is one of those books with easy steps that really ease personal suffering. As a parent, it serves as a tool to provide lessons to our children.

If you do not own this book, I recommend you add it to your library. Each time I read it, it resonates differently with me, depending on what is going on in my life at the time. It has been an enormously helpful tool.

Ruiz explains each agreement in detail with many compelling reasons to follow the steps. Here are the basics. Follow these four steps daily, and you will release yourself from suffering and pain. Easy, right? *Nope!*

But trying is well worth the effort.

**First Agreement**—Be impeccable with your word: "Speak with integrity, say only what you mean."

**Second Agreement**—Don't take anything personally: "Nothing others do is because of you."

**Third Agreement**—Don't make assumptions: "Ask questions and express what you really want."

**Fourth Agreement**—Always do your best: "You will avoid self-judgment, self-abuse, and regret."

An example of how these lessons apply to our children was illustrated when Devin was being teased at school when he was ten. It upset him, but I reminded him of the second agreement: Don't take anything personally. Applying that rule is not an easy change for our minds to make, especially for children. But when you break it down for them, they can learn incredible life lessons from an early age. Those children at my son's school were projecting something on to him just like adults often do in certain situations (road rage in heavy traffic, for example). It was not that these boys, or even the angry drivers in heavy traffic, were doing anything abnormal. This type of stuff happens all the time. However, our acceptance of what others do and whether we take it on is 100 percent on us to decide.

As parents, we could look at all the agreements and agree they are applicable in all our lives, but one agreement hit home for me on my first read of the book. It was a concept I had never considered and one I feel all children should be made aware of and taught from an early age. It was agreement four: Always do your best.

A story I tell my children about one of my many failures in high school illustrates the importance of always doing your best. (By the way, children love to hear about their parents' mistakes while growing up. It makes you, as the parent, more real and relatable.) My failure story was from an athletics carnival (a sports day). I was having a "too cool for school day," and I had to run the 100-meter dash. I was fast way back then, but not in the mood to run, nor would winning do anything for me after that moment. I decided to wing it and play it cool. (I think there was a cute boy involved, but I can neither confirm nor deny this.) The teacher said to me before the race, "Just do your best." I scoffed at her and ran with a bit of a low effort. I lost.

After, I saw the girl who came in first and realized I was usually faster than her. It dawned on me that I could have won. I still think about that day and have not let it go. (Don't get me wrong; I am not losing sleep over this, but here I sit writing about it in this book.) I am held in time at that moment of not doing my best. Now, if I had decided to do my best and lost, that would have been fine. I could have let it go. But I did not do my best, so I wonder if I would have won if I had. Even now, more than twenty-five years later, I still wonder.

Doing your best, and teaching children to do their best, at the end of the day, is all about the child. Not the parents, not the teachers, only that young, developing child! I wish I had understood this lesson in high school. I would have tried much harder, and started trying much sooner.

### The Five Love Languages

A friend of ours, an Army chaplain named Ron, gave us Gary Chapman's *The Five Love Languages* years before we actually took the time to read it. That is unfortunate because understanding how humans communicate love would have helped Deric and me skip over some of the rough spots in our marriage.

The five love languages came into our family during an incredibly stressful time. We had just moved from Kansas to Washington State. We were to be there a few weeks before Deric deployed to Iraq for a year. We had a six-month-old, a two-year-old, and a brand-new house filled with hundreds of packed boxes containing everything we owned. The urgency of getting the house in order before Deric was deployed was, as you can imagine, stressful.

All I wanted to do was spend time with Deric. I wanted him to sit with me and have coffee in the morning. I was okay with sorting the house out on my own when he left; spending time together was my number one priority.

Deric, however, was all over the house, painting, putting pictures up, unpacking boxes, hanging curtain rails, organizing as much as he could. His goal was to set me and the house up 100 percent so when he left, I would not have to do anything around the house. I see now that he was being super-sweet, but at the time, I did not. I just wanted time with him before he left.

All I saw in my fuzzy, stressed mind was him not wanting to spend time with me. It caused us to argue and not see each other's viewpoint. To him, I was utterly illogical. How could I not see how much he loved me by how much he was doing for me? With both of us on completely different pages, and neither feeling loved by the other, he left for Iraq. I am embarrassed to say this, but it was almost a relief to see him go.

While in Iraq, another chaplain gave him *The Five Love Languages* to read. The second time around, I think we got the hint. Deric called me as soon as he started reading it, laughing. "Read the book Ron gave us," he said. "Read it." I did, and also burst out laughing, finally understanding what was so funny.

In the book, Chapman explains that just as we all communicate with spoken language, either German, English, French, etc., we also communicate love with a specific type of "love language." Each of us speaks our own unique dialect when it comes to love languages, not really understanding what anyone else is "saying," and then we wonder why we do not feel fulfilled in relationships. We need someone to speak our specific love language; otherwise, we simply do not feel loved.

Chapman describes the five love languages in easy-to-read chapters that explain the concept way better than I could. You can take an online test to see what love language you speak, but I absolutely recommend reading the book too.

Here are the five love languages:

1.  Words of Affirmation—express love through words and compliments
2.  Acts of Service—any action that eases burden and responsibility
3.  Quality Time—undivided and focused attention spent on someone
4.  Gifts—giving/getting gifts of thoughtfulness
5.  Physical Touch—non-sexual touch that fortifies your presence

For me to feel loved, I need time—have a coffee or a drink and spend time with me (quality time). For Deric to feel like he is giving love, he does things for people (acts of service). We speak opposite love languages. It is like he speaks Spanish and I speak French.

I had to change my ways, how I communicated love, and start doing things that were not natural for me to do to fill Deric's "love tank," and he had to take time from his acts of service to spend time with me to fill my "love tank." Reminders of each other's love language is something we still use in our relationship, and even now, after many years, he always has a cup of coffee with me each morning—doing nothing but chatting and listening. It drives him crazy, but he is speaking my love language, and our relationship is stronger because of it.

What makes the love languages concept especially relevant to parents, besides having a better relationship with your spouse, is that it also applies to children. Chapman wrote a second book called *Five Love Languages for Children*. It was a similar concept, except children carry all five love languages until they mature and gravitate toward one or two like adults. I took Chapman's advice and started to implement each one every day. That is, I started to do things that demonstrated love to my children in each of the languages. I immediately noticed the children were calmer and happier about playing on their own. I committed to them every day, going through a checklist in my mind.

Acts of service is an easy one with children. Making meals, tucking them into bed, helping solve a kid problem. Physical touch is natural and easy as well. Holding hands, snuggles on the couch, patting on the head after doing something good, kisses on the forehead, more snuggles in bed at night, and of course, the constant clamoring and hanging on you at every opportunity.

Quality time and gifts are a bit more interesting. Just sitting on the floor helping my young children build a puzzle would fill their love tanks. When I noticed them starting to whine or act up, I would sit down and play with them. After the quality time came to a natural end, I was able to move on to whatever job I needed to do, like making dinner, etc. They felt loved, and I got time to do what needed to be done.

For gifts, sometimes I just drew a picture or picked a flower for them (just like children instinctively do for us). Their faces would light up immediately. I did not need to buy them stuff. A child's gift does not have to be purchased.

Then, at the end of the day, by bedtime, we had two calm little people whose love tanks were full and who felt loved and safe. That helped them stay in their beds all night and not come crawling into mine searching for more physical touch or quality time. Another win-win. I am very grateful to Chapman for writing the book and to Ron for introducing it to us; it changed our lives. I truly hope it will do the same for you.

## THE CIRCLE OF TRUST

Have you ever seen the movie *Meet the Parents*? If you have not, you should. In the movie, there is an overbearing father played by Robert De Niro. De Niro's character had "The Circle of Trust," something I loved and implemented in our family after seeing the movie. It was meant to be a joke, but the more I thought about it, the more I thought, *But we need a circle of trust, too.* So just like that, our family's circle of trust was born.

My children have asked everything in the circle of trust. Sometimes they have used it as a safe place to vent about something or someone—a friend who is being a jerk or a teacher they just cannot stand. Sometimes the circle of trust is used to test boundaries and see if there are really no consequences. It is not uncommon in my home to have the kids start a conversation saying "circle of trust" before they speak. Just yesterday, my ten-year-old Devin used it to tell me what ADIDAS stood for (At Dinner I Did a Shit). Don't you just love ten-year-old boys? He just wanted to share a joke with a swear word he heard at school with me. And I was happy he could, as it also gives us a window into what they are hearing and seeing outside the home. This might seem a bit silly and frivolous now, but over time, and with constant use, the circle of trust can be extremely useful to a parent.

Imagine a space in a child's life where they can say anything. I mean *anything*! Nothing is off-limits, and more importantly, nothing said in the circle of trust is judged, punished, or reprimanded. There are zero consequences for anything said in the circle of trust. It is a place in the home where any question can be asked, or if they have that "thing" they want to say, there is space to voice it. It has sometimes left me giggling under a face of absolute calm, and sometimes I end up like a deer in headlights, answering, "Ah?"

Let us project forward to when our children are in their teens experiencing difficult life changes and have something they want to discuss, but are afraid to because of the possible consequences. If it is said in the circle of trust, there are no consequences. For the last ten to fifteen years, the circle of trust has been a safe place, without repercussions, for them to share and say what they want, so it will be a safe place now. We start opening the lines of communication while they are young (maybe five years old) so when they are teens and young adults and need real help, they always have a safe, proven place to come first.

When our children are offered drugs by their friends, become addicted to drugs later in life, feel they are ready to have sex as teenagers, become pregnant while at college, get bullied online, are sexually harassed by their boss, become confused about a moral dilemma, are touched inappropriately and warned not to tell anyone, or anything horrible or testing for a maturing mind, they will always have a safe place within the circle of trust to talk about these very difficult situations, without consequences. If you have that space established in your home, and it has been proven safe for the entirety of that child's life, whatever negativity may come into their lives, they have a tool for getting help from their parents, without consequence or punishment, during the most difficult times in their life—true help, from the people who love them the most. Ultimately, I think this is what we all want as parents, to help our children when they need it most. Even though, for now, our circle of trust is used for our ten-year-old to tell fart and poop stories, later, things will get less gross and more real.

### TRUTHFUL? KIND? NECESSARY? ASK THE GUARDS!

I heard this story a few years ago, but for the life of me, I cannot remember where it originated. Regardless, it is an excellent tool because, on occasion, I get the urge to voice my opinion on something, and I am stopped by the memory of this story and the rules that come with it.

Here is how I explain the story to my children:

Imagine you have three guards in your throat. (I always give them a visual aid and explain what the guards look like. In my story, the three guards are old Romans with iron helmets, spears, and shields.) Each guard controls one word—truth, kind, and necessary. When you start to speak, make sure what you have to say passes through each guard in your throat before the words come out.

First Guard: Truthful. Is what you say truthful? If so, your words may move on to the second guard. If not, stop there.

Second Guard: Kind. Is what you say kind? If so, your words may move on to the third guard. If not, stop there.

Third Guard: Necessary. Is what you have to say necessary at this moment? If so, move forward and speak. If not, you are not allowed to say those words.

If your words cannot pass through all the guards, do not say them.

Children can understand the basics of this story and visualize it through their imaginations. Two years ago, while walking with my children on the boardwalk of Virginia Beach, Devin made a comment about someone walking by. In my view, it was not a comment he should have voiced. Reminding him of the story, we went through the guards. Was it truthful? Yes, maybe it was to him. Was it kind? Nope. Therefore, the words should not have got past the kind guard. It was an excellent opportunity to walk and talk to him with a real-life situation where the guards come into play at that moment. I have found that these types of learning moments come up often throughout childhood. When it happens, I simply refer to the Roman guards story, and the kids immediately know they were in the wrong.

I must admit that, even as an adult, the necessary guard is the one who helps me the most. Even today, someone said something I could have very easily added my opinion to, but it was not necessary. Often, our ego needs to add to conversations to build our contribution at the moment. Most of the time, it is not necessary, and therefore, should not be said.

The best part about this lesson is that it applies to both children and parents. Then, when you fail and let some not so necessary or kind words pass through your throat, you can tell your children, and they will understand immediately. Of course, use the circle of trust for this admission; then it again proves the circle works, is active, and parents make mistakes too. Learning is a lifelong process. We all, children and parents, have to ensure our guards are working.

## PERCEPTION IS EVERYTHING

One of my dearest friends, Tiziana, and her beautiful daughter live in Copenhagen, Denmark. I have visited her many times over the years, and on each visit, it has become clearer how differently the Danes raise their children. Specifically, how their babies nap in the day.

If you visit Denmark, which I highly recommend (it is so beautiful), the first thing you might notice is, outside coffee shops, there are carriages (strollers) lined up everywhere. They are much bigger than regular American strollers and are parked outside in the cold Danish air. The shocking part is there are babies in the carriages, asleep while their parents are in the warm coffee shop catching up with friends. Babies in Denmark sleep outside, and parents only bring them in for a nap when temperatures reach what they consider too cold. (What too cold is in Denmark, I am not sure, but I bet it is seriously cold.) They park the carriages outside the shop's windows (in sight, of course), wrap them up warm, and leave them there to sleep. Around the city, carriages are parked outside apartment buildings, daycares, restaurants, and coffee shops! From an outsider's perspective, it is absolutely ludicrous. But from a Danish perspective, it is completely normal.

In many countries, someone would call the authorities in a flash if you did this, but in Denmark, this is it how they do it. Why? Because that is how it is done. They believe inside, in the heat, there are more germs, and too much heat is not suitable for babies to breathe. So, all wrapped up, they are left in the healthy, but sometimes cold, Danish air.

Another observation about Danish parenting that astounded me was that many of the babies were left crying in their carriages... for a long time. During one visit to Tiziana's, she had to knock on her apartment neighbor's door because their baby had been crying outside their apartment for so long. The neighbor opened the door, said, "*Tak*" (Thank you), and brought the baby inside—all calm and without issue. The Danish leave the babies crying to strengthen their lungs. One Danish woman explained this parenting method to me by simply saying, "Babies cry; that's what they do."

If I did not understand this custom or culture from their perspective, I would have instantly thought they were terrible parents. And, apparently, other people would think the same thing because a few weeks ago, just as I was preparing to write this chapter, Tiziana told me a Danish mom in New York City had been arrested for leaving her carriage outside a New York City coffee shop with her baby in it. This story was all over the Danish news, so it was quite a big deal.

In an Australian Outback adventure, I had a real aha! moment. Our camp had no cellphone reception, no internet, and no TVs. We had a little campsite with some glamping tents set up. In the tent next to us was a Danish family. They had two small boys and a baby in a carriage. When the family went into their tent, they left the baby in the carriage outside in the shade of the tent with a fitted fly net covering it. The baby started to cry, and I watched from the tent next door. I realized if I did not understand this custom or culture, I would have thought them terrible parents by leaving the baby outside while the family was inside. But they were great parents, parenting as their culture teaches.

The parenting lesson here is simple: Everyone parents differently. We cannot judge, point at, or criticize others for how they parent. They are most likely doing their very best from a cultural or personal perspective, and their way is probably different from yours.

Another perspective lesson came while I was in the United States, living in Olympia, Washington. Deric was deployed at the time, his second twelve-month tour in Iraq. Deric always said he would call when he could; unfortunately, phone calls were scattered month to month and rare at best. I could never predict when the calls would come, and our being in completely different time zones with a ten-hour difference did not help. One particular day, I went to the grocery store during a nap gap (those gaps between naps are a big thing in a parent's life). While in the store, I grabbed a cart, put both kids in it, and off we went as quickly as I could to get our food for the week. Halfway through my shop, my husband called. Hooray! Oh, shit…I have to finish my shopping in the nap gap! I was too far into my shopping to stop, and naptime was coming closer by the minute. I explained to Deric what was happening and that we would have to walk and talk. Not the best of situations, but we would both have to take it. I carried on shopping, holding the phone to my ear while the kids sat patiently and quietly in the cart as they had been told to do. (Expectations for the kids were set immediately when Deric's call came in. They knew they had to be quiet and sit still.)

While shopping and speaking with Deric, a woman kept passing me on opposite sides of the aisle. Each time we passed each other, she would shake her head at me and roll her eyes in the most obvious and unflattering way. I did not have time to deal with her rudeness and carried on with my exceptionally rare and always special phone call. But she continued to roll her eyes and make her tut-tut sounds as we moved past each other, over and over, aisle after aisle. As I arrived at the cashier, Deric said he had to go. I told him I loved him and to be safe, ended the call, and began putting my shopping on the conveyor belt. Seeing I was now off the phone, the eye-rolling, tut-tut woman felt the need to come tell me what she thought of my parenting.

"What is it with you young mothers today? (I was happy she said young—bright side.) You feel it is more important to have a random conversation on a cellphone than give your children any attention!" All said, of course, with a very snooty, "I am a better mother than you" attitude.

She was very fortunate my "give-a-shit-meter" was at an all-time low. I had actually slept the night prior (four full hours in a row!), and the last kind of behavior I wanted my kids to learn from me was yelling at strangers. Instead of telling her to…well, you get it, I asked her calmly if she supported the troops. She answered yes straight away, with some pride in her voice. I told her I was talking to my husband, deployed in Iraq, who rarely had access to a phone and could not schedule calls. I thanked her for supporting the troops and wondered out loud if that support extended to their families who were doing their best under incredibly difficult circumstances. Her face dropped. She walked away embarrassed. I hope she grew in that moment and never felt the need to call out a mom again.

We can never judge a mom or dad in a moment. You do not know where they are in their day, week, or year. You have no idea what has happened before or after, and one glimpse into their lives does not tell you the whole story. Your perspective might not be entirely accurate. But if the judgment has already happened (I get it…we all judge a little) and you still feel the need to say something, check with the guards first.

## TRADITIONS

Traditions are a huge part of every culture around the world. Some traditions are tied to a nation, tribe, or religion. Some traditions are passed down through the family. Some traditions, however, are new, brought into the family by necessity, and then never seem to go away. Whatever they are or wherever they come from, traditions are important for feeling safe, included, and normal in a family. I did not understand the power of traditions until we let a few slip.

One of our family traditions started when we lived in Kansas, when Deric was working on his master's degree, and we were saving to buy a house. We were in a spending freeze where we only bought what we needed, did not eat out, and saved every penny we could. At that time, I had a toddler and a newborn, so it was easier to cook at home. The kids were at the age where anything they did was new and fun, so eating out was more difficult than making a meal at home. But once a week, every Sunday for a year straight, we went out for ice cream. We called it "Sundae Sundays." It was the only unnecessary spending we did each week. Rain or shine, every Sunday we went out for ice cream. And we still do; to this day, we have a family Sundae Sunday each and every week. The kids hold it so close to their hearts that if we forget (which has happened once or twice), it ends in tears and broken hearts. It is also the only day of the week they get ice cream, which makes it even more special.

I have friends who have a big Sunday family lunch every week. No matter what is happening, the entire family comes home (even adult children) to be there—it is their family tradition. It is non-negotiable time. Other friends from the United States have Thanksgiving at a certain family member's house every year, eat the exact same meal, and play football in the backyard. Regardless of where the traditions come from, make them your own.

What are your family traditions?

_____

_____

_____

_____

_____

_____

_____


What family traditions can you start?

_____

_____

_____

_____

_____

_____

_____

**LESSONS LEARNED**

- The Tantrum Cookie—make the parenting lessons memorable.

- When you share, you get more.

- Every toy belongs to the house.

- If you give, you receive at the same time.

- Teach children to think of others each day.

- Volunteering is an incredible example for children to see and experience.

- *The Four Agreements.*

- Children love to hear about their parents' mistakes.

- *The Five Love Languages.*

- The Circle of Trust.

- Truthful, Kind, Necessary? Ask the Guards!

- Learning is a lifelong process.

- Perception is everything—Danish napping.

- Everyone parents differently.

- Never judge a mom or dad in the moment.

- Traditions provide security, belonging, and normalcy, a powerful gift we can give our children.

# CHAPTER 11

# PARENTING FORESIGHT FROM FIJI

*"Alone we can do so little; together we can do so much."*

— *Helen Keller*

Have you ever had your parenting ideals flipped upside down and felt like you had to start all over again? What would you do if you saw a whole new angle you had never thought about? Well, that is exactly what happened to me in Fiji.

## BIG LOVE

Traveling to Fiji offered Deric and me one of the most significant parenting lessons ever. On a whim, we booked this once-in-a-life-time trip one week before leaving. Fiji is a go-to destination for Australians since the flight is only a few hours from Sydney, and oddly enough, it is cheaper to fly to Fiji than coast to coast in Australia. So we went.

When you step off the plane in Fiji, you just feel love. I do not mean warm, fuzzy, sweet love; I am talking about heart-wrenching, in-your-face love.

As we waited to get our rental car, we saw some elderly men parked in a no parking zone on the side of the road. They were all laughing and sharing stories in a relaxed and happy atmosphere...on the side of the road, mind you. It was like nothing I had ever seen. The happiness that oozed out of them was mesmerizing. We stood and watched this jovial gathering in no rush to move on ourselves. And when we did finally decide to drive away, we got big smiles from the men, a friendly wave, and an energetic, "*Bula!*"

All you hear around Fiji is "*Bula!*" being shouted from every corner. *Bula* is Fijian for hello, but it is also a heartfelt blessing, similar to *Aloha* in Hawaii but shouted with impassioned force from the deepest parts of the heart. We found that most Fijians rarely let anyone go past them without giving them a heartfelt blessing. From the men hanging out on the side of the road, to retailers, to kids playing in the village, and even to Elliot the pool bartender, who would greet us with the generosity of his full heart. It was all eye-opening...but confusing. How could everyone here be so happy and grateful?

Outside of the glamourous hotel and tourist areas you see on all the brochures, Fiji is a bit rundown, with evidence of poverty all around. Most people live simply, some have cars, some do not, and homes are very small and modest. Why did these people who had so little look and act as if they had so much?

One morning at our hotel, our waitress at breakfast was happily chatting with our family. She told us her children lived on a different island, and she was preparing to go see them soon. Her journey would involve a long bus ride to a port and two separate boat rides overnight. (I am not sure what kind of boat this was, but I am sure it was not fancy.) How was she so happy about her life even living away from her family and with an upcoming all-day bus and boat trip? Every day when we went for breakfast, I would secretly find the table she was working just so I could have more chats and ask her more questions about her life. What I noticed after each question and each day was that all her answers were centered in gratitude. Not just gratitude but *gratitude!* She kept saying, "But I'm happy"...and meant it.

Thinking that all the happiness and gratitude might just be coming from the hotel staff for the lucky tourists staying there, we got in our rental car and went out driving. On most of our family holidays or explorations, we usually schedule a "follow your nose day." You see, my husband, being a well-disciplined Army officer, is a planner who must schedule everything. (Although annoying, it is useful, I admit.) Meanwhile, I am the "less structured" partner in our relationship, and I like to do things as I "feel" them, not be restricted by time and schedules. So, the "scheduled" activity pleases Deric, and the "follow your nose" pleases me. (Win, win.) To follow your nose means you have no plans and go where your nose points you. Everyone in the family gets a chance to lead with their nose and see where life takes us for the day. It's a fun and exciting way to explore new places and get off the beaten path wherever you may be. (Kids love this, by the way. It makes them feel like they have a say in the trips and making family decisions!)

**FIRE!**

On our "follow your nose" drive around the island with all its beautiful surroundings, we found ourselves on a side road headed toward a village where we saw smoke from a distance. Then we saw a small house was on fire. The fire was bellowing out of every door and window. The houses in the village were concrete and close together, so it seemed that most of the fire was coming from everything inside the home. We carefully drove past the house to avoid the lone fire truck and two firefighters. It looked like the entire village was in the streets. There must have been about 100 people out on the road, standing around the house, talking with each other, and watching the firefighters. As we drove past the burning house, we saw the owners watching helplessly from the side of the road—my heart broke. I had the urge to do something, but I did not know what I could possibly do.

At that sad moment on that unnamed road in a small village some-where in Fiji, my family learned a valuable lesson. As we watched what we thought was a tragedy unfolding in front of us, everyone in the village watching the fire seemed unusually calm. No one was freaking out, children were playing soccer across the street, and when we looked closely, we actually saw some people smiling. Men and woman were speaking calmly, while sitting on the sidewalk like nothing was going on. What? My brain could not process this. I wanted to shout out the window of the car, "Can't you see the house is on fire?"

Then, out of nowhere, unexpectedly, the group sitting on the curb watching the fire stood up as we drove past and not only waved to us, not only smiled at us, but each and every one of them shouted a heartfelt, "*Bula!*" as we glided by. Some of the kids even stopped playing soccer to run with the car and scream, "*Bula!*" They expected nothing; they just wanted to say hello to a family of strangers driving by, share a smile, and give a blessing. All of this, as the house contin-ued to burn. I was dumbfounded. What just happened?

Later, after we found our way back to the hotel, I asked every local I could about this event, trying to figure out how this type of commu-nity works. The answers I got over and over from everyone I spoke with were surprising. People have each other, they have a village, they have little attachment to material things, and lastly, most im-portantly, they all live in gratitude. These lovely islanders explained that the people whose house had burnt knew they would get support from the community, so why worry? They were grateful, and they knew they would be just fine in the end. This was true detachment from material things in action, and it carried no anxiety, concern, or discomfort. These wonderful people knew what was important, and it was not what was on fire.

## EVERYONE GETS BITTEN BY ANTS

This happiness and gratitude for everything concept of life intrigued me to my core, so on my quest to find out more, I spoke to as many people as I could. I wanted what they had. I wanted to live an anxiety-free life too. I wanted to feel gratitude in every moment and situation I found myself in. I wanted to give my children and family what Fijians gave their kids.

A few days later, Deric decided to hire a boat to take us around to the outer islands, surf spots, and to snorkel at some reefs. Don't be too impressed; nothing costs a lot in Fiji. When the day came for our outer island tour, we were told to be on the beach at 8:00 a.m., and the boat would meet us there. Sure enough, as we walked down the beach in the morning to start our adventure, a cool looking red, orange, and yellow boat came out of the beautiful blue and turquoise waters and drove right up to us on the beach. We were welcomed with a warm, *"Bula!"* from two men on the boat named Ice and Wise.

Wise was precisely that, and I wondered how his parents could have known the day he was born that he would grow up to embody the very definition of his name. During our all-day adventure on the boat, I asked Ice and Wise a million questions and found out Wise had lived in this area of Fiji all his life. Wise was quiet, but you could feel he was a man who knew exactly who he was. Calm, strong, and well…wise. He was in his late sixties, knew every inch of the waterways, and seemed to know everyone on the islands as well. He had volunteered in the community to plant trees on the sandbars to develop them into full-blown islands over ten to twenty years. As we sailed past the sandbars he had worked on, he showed us ones his father and grandfather had developed decades before.

Ice was much younger, mid- to late-twenties, and well…cool as ice. He was Lenny Kravitz cool! When our boat got to a good surf spot, he paddled out with Deric to catch a few waves while Wise, the kids, and I stayed on the boat, enjoying the beauty all around us and watching them surf from the boat. You could tell Ice knew these waters; he was a master for sure. By the end of the day hanging out with Ice and Wise, I felt I could ask a deeper question. I threw my question at Ice, the chattier of the two. I asked him why all Fijians seem so happy and grateful.

His answer changed my life.

Ice told me a story about him and his father that happened when Ice was just five years old. Ice, his father, and others from the village were traveling deep into the Fijian forests to hunt wild pigs. A few hours into the trip, young Ice started getting bitten by ants. Big ants were all over his legs, biting him, and they were hurting him badly. Ice started crying, whining, and complaining to his father. After listening to the whining and complaining for a while, Ice's father grabbed him by the scruff of his neck and pulled him aside.

He told Ice that everyone in the forest was getting bitten by ants, and everyone there was in pain and irritated by the ants just like he was. He explained that everyone gets bitten by ants in the forest, and if everyone whined, complained, and cried, the entire village would be miserable. He went on to make it clear that our actions affect everyone around us, and that our constant need to remind people of our pain will alert everyone around us to their pain. "We all get bitten by ants, but think about others first before you whine about it," Ice's dad concluded.

Think about that for a minute.

If we believed that our actions, words, bad moods, complaints, negative remarks, and irritations affected everyone around us, would we still act the same way? Imagine if we all deeply cared how what we said affected those around us. How would we act then? How would we adjust the way we speak to and teach our children? What if we taught this lesson to ourselves first, then our children—like young

Ice, who learned this lesson at age five. Imagine for a moment how different our world would look if we considered those around us before thinking about our own pain and need to spread it. Imagine how our children, as teens and adults, would think before reacting and speaking. How much calmer and more at ease with life's difficulties would they feel? How much calmer and more at ease with life's difficulties would our family and community be? It is not impossible. I saw a culture where people lived like this every day. They were happy, grateful, and caring people—all because they taught their children that everyone gets bitten by ants.

## LESSONS LEARNED

- Teach children to deal with what is going on around them.

- Teach children to think of others in their family and community; this is crucial to children's development and the family's wellbeing.

- Thinking of others encourages empathy, sharing, and kindness in a beautiful way. Imagine if we all learned from the beginning that everyone is getting bitten by ants.

- As a parent, you determine the very first lessons your children learn.

- Regularly teach lessons that expand from family, to community, to culture.

CHAPTER 12

# SMALL THINGS...THAT ARE BIG THINGS

*"Lack of boundaries invites lack of respect."*

— *Anonymous.*

## DON'T RAISE AN ASSHOLE

A couple of years ago in Virginia, United States, I saw my friend Amy at school dropoff. She had that look on her face like something significant had just happened, and I could tell the morning had started badly. I asked if she was okay, and she said, "Well, I just told my kids they are assholes; that's how my day started!"

I burst out laughing. I loved that Amy had taken a step back as a parent and looked at her kids from another perspective. Reality. I loved that she had the guts to call them out and shock them with the truth. I loved that she saw the beginnings of behavior in her children that she did not approve of and nipped it in the bud immediately. I vowed to myself on that day that I, too, would call my kids assholes when the time came. In that one, very funny, but very real moment, Amy gave me permission to call my children out, to not live in the fake reality that all our kids are perfect human beings. And believe me when I tell you that I have called out my kids many times already.

195

The interesting part about this story is that Amy's kids are great! I would have never considered them naughty by any definition of the term. But when Amy saw a negative behavior starting to pop up in her kids, she stopped it there and then. Amy's children, just like all children, will test behavioral boundaries. They are trying to gain independence and strength as individuals through childhood experimentation (aka: acting like assholes). We also have to remember that just because kids act up does not make them bad kids. They need someone to show them what is acceptable and what is not. They find this guidance through childhood experimentation. That is our job. They only become true assholes once we, as parents, let them act like assholes too many times.

## BOUNDARIES

Boundaries = freedom for everyone in the family.

A team of architects from Mississippi State University conducted an experiment to see the physical and psychological effects of fences around preschool playgrounds.

The findings showed when playgrounds had no fences, children were inclined to assemble around the teacher and were hesitant to wander. On playgrounds with fences, the children were more inclined to run around the whole playground, feeling free to explore.

Once I had kids, I finally understood this study and its results more clearly. The more boundaries I put on my children, the safer they felt, and the calmer they behaved. As they grew, I added more boundaries, slowly and consistently, based on their developing levels of maturity and responsibility. And at each phase, they were calm and more comfortable because boundaries had always been a part of their lives.

When my mother-in-law found out I was pregnant with my first child, she gave me a tremendous lesson in parenting reality. She explained that from the moment you have a baby, you would forever be letting that child go. This idea stayed with me, and I found it to be more and more accurate as the years went on. From the moment you hold your bundle of joy for the first time, you are handing your child to other people, letting your child walk alone, sending them to school, letting them go to sleepovers, allowing them to go to movies with friends, then off to college, and so it continues. You have to let your children do more, independently, their entire lives.

But the story about the boundaries also stayed with me. Boundaries make us feel safe. A railing on a staircase makes us feel safe—that is a boundary. So, when bringing up a child to be strong, independent, and inquisitive, we need to be sure to set boundaries. Now, do not confuse boundaries with suffocation. Boundaries should feel warm and safe, not stifling and limiting. We want our children to feel free to explore their lives as they grow and mature. To do that, we have to set boundaries that give the feeling of both safety and freedom.

Spend a moment thinking about the boundaries you have in place for your children. Once you have listed them, look to see if they encourage a feeling of safety. If not, how could they be changed?

Here are some examples:

Toddlers:

- Hold my hand when crossing the street.
- Do not play with the curtains or curtain strings.

Bigger kids:

- Stay where you can hear me call for you.
- Stay where I can see you.
- Wear a helmet when riding your bike, skateboard, or rollerblades.
- School day bedtime is 9:00 p.m.

Teenagers:

- Text me when you get to your friend's house.
- Curfew is 11 p.m.

_____

_____

_____

_____

_____

_____

_____

Are you ready to bring more boundaries into your family's life? If yes, what would they be?

_____

_____

_____

_____

_____

_____

## NO FIGHTING

One of my most cherished high school friends from South Africa is Janine. She is the loveliest, kindest person you could meet. Janine has a brother James two years younger than her, and they are best friends. James and Janine had a bond as siblings and friends everyone admired. If I went to their house as a teen, they always showed the most incredible respect for each other. She never complained about him being an annoying brother, and he always spoke proudly of her. I knew if she ever had to choose between her brother and me, there would be no contest. He would win for sure.

As they grew up and life became more real, they got even closer. I watched as we all became adults, how they loved and respected each other through adult issues. I watched how they did or did not approve of each other's boyfriends or girlfriends, and how they would stand together when times got tough. I watched how, over the years, they were always there for each other, no matter how difficult the problem. Today, they are in their forties. When I spoke to Janine a few days ago, she told me they had spoken twice that day. I knew the relationship they had was the kind I wanted my kids to have.

In contrast, I met a mother once whose children were all adults in their thirties and had just returned from a weekend get-together as a family. When I commented on how fabulous it must have been to go on a family weekend getaway with her adult children, she stopped me in mid-sentence and said, "It was hell! All the kids did was fight, argue, and bicker, just like they always have." I felt terrible for her.

As parents, we hear so often that "all siblings fight," so we take it as the absolute truth. Usually, because we fought with our siblings, or we do not know a family that does not fight. Regardless, this does not have to be the case. I genuinely believe if we teach respect to our children from an early stage, we can guide them to have differences with siblings without fighting. When we let children fight with each other, they get used to acting that way. As parents, we have to teach children how to speak to others, including their brothers and sisters. Janine's parents did exactly that; they would not allow James and Janine to fight, so they did not.

Would you ever have shouted at a teacher or principal at your school? Why? Because they would not let you. Would you ever swear at your parents? Why? Because they would not allow you to. You speak to people as they allow you to speak to them. You speak to people as you have been taught to speak to them.

So why do we, as parents, feel it is okay for our children to fight and speak badly to each other?

I implemented a "no fighting" rule when my children were three and five and had started bickering and fighting with each other. I realized this behavior was becoming normalized, and thought of my dear friend Janine and her brother. My kids needed to be taught now how to treat each other because it was not happening naturally. I explained (in my scary mom voice) that they were the only two people in each other's lives who would be there for the rest of their lives, and they were never allowed to disrespect each other. Ever! I explained they are too special to each other as brother and sister to fight, and that they had to be able to rely on each other for their entire lives. With such a special relationship required of siblings, you cannot fight. Period.

And since that time, they seldom have. (Notice I said seldom.) On rare occasions, things have become heated, but I have immediately intervened and reminded them of the rule. If the rule is enforced every time the rule is broken, kids typically do not push it. Instead, they learn ways to get their point across without fighting.

## NAGGING—YES, I'M GOING THERE

Once after a frustrating day of parenting—you know those days, the ones where you feel like all you do is correct your kids—I decided to step back and listen to myself speak on an average day at home. At the end of the day, I thought to myself, *Goodness, you are annoying.* It is unquestionably overwhelming to think that, as parents, we must teach these small, innocent humans all they need to know to become adults in a very short time. Feeling overwhelmed, we often turn to nagging to get all the required life lessons taught in that very short period.

What happens if we hear a noise in the background all day long? We eventually block that noise out. Our nagging voice is the same, and kids will eventually block our noise out too. We hear parents all the time saying, "My kids don't hear a word I say," and that is probably the truth. Nagging voices get tuned out. Do you want your kids to always hear you? Then stop nagging.

Choose one or two issues a day you want to focus on, and let everything else go. Yes, let everything else go. If you are working with little ones on keeping food on the table, teach that lesson during their messy lunch. Later, you can work on looking both ways before crossing the street. Done for the day! Do not mention the toys left all over the house, or the messy room, or anything else—just those two lessons.

The next day, remind them about the food and walking across the street, and then work on taking plates to the sink. The urge to cram every life lesson into our children is strong, but stop yourself. Take your time, and use a slower, no nagging approach. You may notice yourself becoming more relaxed, and they will hear you. All those essential life lessons will eventually be taught. And yes, you might have to repeat yourself a few times throughout their childhood, but the lessons will be absorbed, and you will not be a nag.

PARENTING TOOLBOX

### Time Out Game—for Younger Children

We all know children can get out of control; I think they are wired that way. Kids always take things too far, get too loud, and then end up breaking something or themselves. If there is more than one kid in the room, a perfectly reasonable game or a completely uneventful day can go from calm and relaxed to bouncing off the walls crazy in seconds. So how do we, as parents, keep playtime fun but reasonable, while not sounding like nags?

Introducing the "Time Out Game." Kids enjoy a firm rule they can easily understand, and time out is exactly that. Despite being primarily used in sports to stop play, time outs work on kids. To a kid, everything is a game, and a parent is like an official, so it matches perfectly. Every time you need to stop a game or activity your children are playing and have a bit of a reset, you shout out, "*Time Out Game!*"

After they stop, and amazingly they do, you can tell them what they need to hear, set them straight, or deal with any issues. For example: "Time Out Game! Hey, guys, let's move away from the glass cabinet behind you and calm down just a bit; got it?" Then you can say, "*Time In Game—go,*" and walk away, letting the game continue. Children immediately realize the game is back on and get right back to playing, but within the new parameters you established.

Just last night before bedtime, the kids started playing and things went from zero to 100 really fast. I used "*Time Out Game!*" (yelled it actually), and like magic, they just stopped and listened. (Please remember, this tool has been used in my house now for ten years, so we are well practiced.) I said something like, "Hey, guys, you need to be in bed in ten minutes, and we need to bring it down a little." Then continued with "*Time In Game...go!*" The pause in their game naturally calmed them down for the few seconds while they listened to me. Then I reminded them it was bedtime and not the middle of the day, and they knew what was expected of them.

The best part about using this tool is that you, as a parent, are not actually stopping their game, just pausing it temporarily, just like a sports official, and then letting the kids play again. You are not the mean mom or dad who always stops kids from having fun. That is a win, win. A win for you as a parent setting new noise, location, safety, or whatever parameters and not looking like the mean mom or dad. And a win for kids who keep playing. Boom! Parenting success with three little words. *Time Out Game.* Say it loud and say it proud…they will hear you.

### Swap Days/Role-Play—for Younger Children

Many years ago, when I was a young college student in South Africa, not even thinking about being a parent, one of my favorite college professors, Ms. Joubert, gave me an incredible tool for my parenting toolbox. It was not her intent to teach parenting, and I surely did not understand it then, but this tool allowed me to see how my parenting was viewed by my children. Ms. Joubert would say, "If you want to see what you understand as a student, then teach it."

Wondering one day if my kids were understanding what I was trying to teach them, I took Ms. Joubert's lesson—if you want to see what your children have learned, let them teach you—and we started swap days. A swap day (or hour—the time is irrelevant) is where you are the children, and they are the parents. Let them look after you. Let them take control. They love this! You have to be okay with relinquishing control for a while. For some people, this could be hard, but the benefits are well worth it.

When you play swap day with your children, you see if they have learned what you are trying to teach them. Let them teach you how to walk across the street, how to deal with a stranger, or how to call 911. You can even let them put you in time out! (You will see how they see you in those parenting moments.) There are so many lessons you can test through play and gain insight into their world. Take note if they shout, nag, or snap at you in these moments, or if they are loving and kind with their words and actions. They will emulate what you do as a parent, or how their daycare center is treating them, because that is all they know. And because it is a game, the kids think they are playing, but you are actually evaluating your parenting skills and the people they spend days with.

When playing swap days in our house, my kids always put me in time out. (Little did they know it is a parent's dream to be put in time out.) I was amazed how, at the end of my time outs, they told me why I was there and then gave me a cuddle and told me how much they loved me. I also noticed, through several iterations of swap days, that my kids offered me food a lot, they pretended to speak on the phone often, and they were always saying they needed to do chores. That was how they saw me. Always busy doing something, always feeding them, and evidently, always on the phone. I know everything I was doing was needed to run a house and be a mom, but playing swap day was a great eye-opener for understanding how my kids saw me. After seeing this, I was able to adjust how I was parenting, and I changed my call times to after their bedtimes.

Specific role-playing can also be a part of swap day. This is where you have your children pretend to be a teacher, coach, daycare provider, or anyone who regularly supervises your children. I used role-playing with my kids because, when I was in elementary school, my teachers used to yell like there was no tomorrow and hit the students with rulers. Seriously, it was out of control. Therefore, as a young girl, I viewed school as violent.

When I was a child, my Great-Aunty Eileen was a teacher in England, and she would come to visit our family in South Africa on holiday. On one visit, when I was about seven, she watched me play "school" with my dolls and teddies. I assumed the role of teacher and began yelling and hitting my teddies on their hands with a ruler. After only a few minutes of role-playing, Eileen said to my mom, "There is a problem at that school, and you should have a look into it."

Always remembering this moment with my great-aunt, I used role-play to see how other adults speak to my kids. I say, "Let's play school; you are (whoever)," and ask them to teach me. I then watched how they spoke and taught me. I was lucky that I only saw a sweet, soft-spoken teacher, and it was a relief to know what was going on in the classroom.

Take time now to think about what lessons your kids can teach you during swap days.

_____

_____

_____

_____

_____

_____

_____

_____

_____

_____

_____

_____

Make a list of who you would like your children to role-play (yourself, teachers, or people in different environments).

_____

_____

_____

_____

_____

### Flying with Kids and Babies

My first international flight with a baby was just seven weeks after Kailey was born. Deric had deployed to Afghanistan for another combat tour the week before, and I wanted to be with my family in South Africa during that first year with a new baby. I flew solo, with a brand-new baby, on an eighteen-hour, direct flight from Virginia to Johannesburg, South Africa. And just in case you do not know, or you might have forgotten, new moms typically do not know what the hell they are doing. Well, that was the case for me anyway.

A new mom, by herself with a seven-week-old baby, on an eighteen-hour international flight. I was nursing at the time, and therefore, the only food source for my baby. During the check-in process at the airlines, I tried to get a bulkhead seat so I could get a crib. Unfortunately, they were already reserved. The airline had given those seats to a few men with long legs, as I discovered walking onto the plane with my baby and all the baby stuff in tow. My daughter and I were put in an aisle seat next to a young man in his early twenties.

As you might guess, he freaked out when he saw me and my baby walk up to the seat and plop down all our baby goodies next to him.

Instead of offering to help, he immediately tried to get out of his seat by stepping over us. He went straight to the hostess to complain, evidently because my existence on this planet with a seven-week-old baby did not fit his personal flight requirements. After a few minutes of discussion, he began yelling.

We all know an upset mama usually activates a baby to be upset too, and you guessed it, my daughter went to baby-crying town. I was not very popular on the plane even before we had taken off. People all around me got more and more upset that I could not control my baby. (How does anyone control a seven-week-old?) I then did the unimaginable. I started nursing right next to this young man in an attempt to calm my daughter down and stop her crying. This, of course, turned his twenty-year-old toddler tantrum with the hostess from a ten to a solid 100.

Completely overwhelmed and upset at this point, I started to break down. The hostess, who was an African mama (full of love and strength), noticed I was upset and overwhelmed. She came over to me, took the crying baby, and said, "Come with me, Mummy. I got baby; you get your bags." She was an angel sent from heaven. This woman took me to the food serving area, and said, "We are moving a few people around. Let me deal with this man. You just wait here and take care of that precious baby." I stood there for a little while, and then she came back to escort me to my new, upgraded seat. When the twenty-year-old tantrum guy saw this, he freaked out again, saying he should be upgraded, not me. I just smiled and thanked him for all his help.

From that day on, I vowed not to stress when it comes to travel. Stress gets you nowhere fast and does not help anyone. As a traveler, you have very little control of your time or what is happening around you. Sometimes, you just have to look on the bright side and trust things will work out.

One particular plane trip from Kansas City, Kansas, to Seattle, Washington, fit that concept exactly. I had a situation where my decision to just "go with the flow" worked out in my favor.

On our move from Kansas to Washington, Deric drove the family car with the cat, cross country, while the kids and I flew. Since Kailey was two years old and Devin was four months, we decided this would be the less stressful, easiest way to get halfway across the country. I arrived at the airport with a toddler, a baby in a car seat, and a carry-on. As we checked in, I saw that not one of our three seats was next to another—we would be in three separate seats on the flight, so I asked if we could fix that. The airline receptionist told me it would have to be done at the gate so they could move some people around. I nodded and went through security. I got to the gate early to give them time to move whoever they needed to move, but there was already a long line in front of the two women working the desk. I stood in line with my kids and eventually got in front of another airline receptionist who could help me. I stood at the tall desk, my kids not in eye view at the time, and explained my situation. "My two small kids and I are sitting in separate rows, and I was hoping you could seat us together." She sighed, and said, "Sometimes it is just not possible to sit with your family on a four-hour flight." Then she told me to go sit down because she could not alter any more seats. "Next!" she yelled over my head.

I calmly went to sit down in the crowded waiting area. I was surprised by the receptionist's answer and mentioned it to a woman sitting next to me, just to make sure I was not crazy. This situation would not go over well on the plane. She immediately freaked out! "Go tell them again," she said very upset. I told her I had, and that I was sure it would all get worked out. "Go with the flow," I told myself.

By the time we boarded, my seating situation had still not been resolved, and when they called for parents with young children to board first, I got up and walked down the gateway. I was first on the plane, so

I put my son in his car seat on the seat that had been assigned to him in row eleven. Then walked to row seventeen and put my two-year-old next to the window. Then walked to row twenty-two and took my seat. The hostess—the same woman as at the desk who had told me moving was not possible—shouted, "Ma'am, ma'am!" over and over. "What are you doing?" Just then, everyone else started boarding. I said rather loudly, "Could you tell the person sitting next to my four-month-old to give him a pacifier when he gets upset, and that he needs feeding in an hour. And tell the person next to my two-year-old that she will stop crying eventually." I am not sure what happened next, but within minutes, there were seats for the kids and me, all in one row. I had no stress or worry. It all worked out.

Each of these stories is just a funny example to remind us that sometimes when we travel, it is not worth getting upset about everything. If we did, we would be upset the entire trip, and that is no fun for us or our children. Traveling is fun, new, and exciting for children. We should not ruin it by stressing and worrying about every problem along the way. Whether it is a short two-hour trip or a seriously long eighteen-hour trip, eventually it will all work out. And on the occasional trip where everything goes wrong, it will eventually end.

## Travel Tips

Since our family travels so often, I get a lot of parents asking me how to travel best with kids. The following are best traveling practices I have picked up along the way. These tips mainly apply to flying, but they can be adapted to all travel: planes, trains, and automobiles.

☐ **Be over-prepared:** Always bring extra clothes. Once, on a ten-hour, overnight flight from Munich to Johannesburg, both my kids got food poisoning from the airport dinner. For nearly the entire flight, both kids were throwing up. It was a colossal mess, and the smell was, as you can imagine, thick and pungent. I felt so bad for everyone around me, but there was nothing I could do. Luckily, on this trip, I was surrounded by amazing people, and I would like to truly thank everyone who supported me on this flight. There is nothing like a group of strangers helping someone out whom they will never see again. Now, I always have spare clothes, wet wipes, and lots of plastic bags. I am over-prepared.

☐ **Take as little entertainment as possible:** This becomes more possible as children age. For young ones, it is very difficult. For older children, one book and an iPad with preloaded games and movies is more than enough. Always download some movies before leaving; if there is no entertainment, you will always have a backup. Be over-prepared, but take as little as possible.

☐ **Bring snacks:** On an international flight, or anything over a mealtime, I have a peanut butter and jelly sandwich in my bag. Most of the time, it goes to my husband, but if the meal is something your kids will not eat, you have an alternate. Some international flights can have international food, and a plane is not a place you want to expand your child's culinary experiences.

☐ **Headphones:** Once your kids are big enough to watch the entertainment or use an iPad, invest in a pair of comfortable headphones. No one wants to hear the show any kid is watching at 3 a.m. The comfortable part is key because, if the headphones hurt your children, they will not wear them, and everyone will get to hear *Baby Shark* for the next three hours.

☐ **Freedom:** Travel is absolute freedom from parental screen time rules for my kids now that they are older. I call it "movie marathon time," where they can watch as much as they like or play games for as long as they like. I do put them to sleep on long flights, but other than that, they have no limitations with entertainment. This is a big deal because, at home, there are many limitations on games and TV time, so this is their little travel perk. The parents' travel perk is having fully entertained kids for as long as you are in the air.

☐ **Learning opportunities:** Teach children how to travel—how to check-in, go through security, find the gate, speak to receptionists, use a passport, or find a train connection. Make the travel a learning experience for the day when you are not with them. It is easy for children to move around the airport with blinders on and not pay attention to what needs to be done. Engage with them during the entire process. Give them the task of getting the family to the gate, remembering the seat numbers, or watching the time. These tasks engage children during what can be a very long day and gives them small challenges to figure out. These tips also work for bus trips, train trips, or reading a map. Travel is a great learning opportunity that will empower your future adult child.

## LESSONS LEARNED

- You have one job as a parent.... Don't raise an asshole.

- Live in reality, and call your kids out when they need it.

- Children feel safer with boundaries.

- Siblings will be with each other for their entire lives. This special relation requires respect, not fighting.

- Nagging voices get blocked out.

- Time Out Game.

- Swap days.

- Traveling with kids—stay calm; it will all work out.

- Traditions provide security, belonging, and normalcy—a powerful gift we can give our children.

# CHAPTER 13

# PARENTING PHILOSOPHIES FROM HAWAII

*"E hele me ka puʻol."*
*"Make every person, place, or condition better than you left it always."*

— *Hawaiian proverb*

W hen traveling, you have two options: Travel like a tourist, or try to experience the real culture. I always try to step out of tourist mode just for a bit to find the authentic culture of wherever I am. Seeing any location as a tourist and then seeing it through local eyes is very different. We have to do all we can to see and understand cultures. I usually say, if you have not had a meal with a local family, in a local house, it is difficult to understand how the country and culture works.

My husband lived part of his life in Hawaii as a child, then went to the University of Hawaii, and later worked in Hawaii as a young man before I met him. He fell in love with the people and culture, and he continues to talk about his time there and the Aloha Spirit. Even on our first date, he talked about Hawaii, its incredible landscapes, beautiful people, and how he wanted to live there again someday. Over the years, when we had an opportunity for a vacation, he always managed to convince me that Hawaii would be the perfect holiday destination—again.

During each visit to Hawaii, I saw something exceptional and understood more of what Deric was trying to explain on our first date. And as I always say, if you put things out there enough, and ask for something with an open heart, you will eventually get it. So, after multiple visits and hundreds of conversations, my husband and I decided to move to Hawaii to live and parent with the Aloha Spirit.

## THE ALOHA SPIRIT

We cannot go any further into the lessons this special place has to offer until we firmly understand the idea of Aloha. This word is known all over the world, usually as a greeting, but it is so much more. It is a lifestyle, a philosophy, a genuine spirit.

One of Hawaii's treasured Kupuna (elders), Auntie Pilahi Paki, described the Aloha Spirit as the coordination of the mind and heart, bringing each person to the self. The Aloha Spirit was and still is a philosophy of native Hawaiians. Which, by itself, is a beautiful way to think about and live your life—mind and heart together. To ensure it was understood by all and maintained in written history, state representatives asked their treasured auntie to explain it further and record it in state law for perpetuity under HRS S5-7.5.

There, she described the Aloha Spirit as:

Akahai—meaning kindness (grace), to be expressed with tenderness

Lokahi—meaning unity (unbroken), to be expressed with harmony

Olu'olu—meaning agreeable (gentle), to be expressed with pleasantness

Ha'aha'a—meaning humility (empty), to be expressed with modesty

Ahonui—meaning patience (waiting for the moment), to be expressed with perseverance

Aloha means mutual regard and affection and extends warmth and caring with no obligation in return. Aloha is the essence of relationships in which each person is essential to every other person for their collective existence. Aloha means to hear what is not said, to see what cannot be seen, and to know the unknowable. These Hawaiian words and their meanings described the character that expresses the beauty and sincerity of the Hawaiian people.

The Aloha Spirit can actually be seen and felt in Hawaii—through random acts of kindness observed every day between strangers, through the smiles and genuine happiness of the locals seen as they live their normal lives and the warm and heartfelt greetings offered from family and friends.

But most importantly, it is something taught from generation to generation—from elders to children, ensuring every generation continues to live by the values and character of their forebears. It is a pure and beautiful example of how to parent your children and live your life.

This parenting and life philosophy does not provide how-to instructions. It does not recommend time outs for bad behavior, star charts for success, or an allowance to show the importance of work.

The Aloha Spirit is a philosophy to live by for children, parents, and the entire community. It provides characteristics and values to teach children. It is one of the loveliest ways to live and parent that I have experienced in all my travels.

## CONNECTORS

When living in Washington State, I met a woman named Susan whose son was in my daughter's preschool. They had just moved from Hawaii, and as preschool moms do, we would usually hang around outside the drop-off area and chat after saying goodbye to our kids. She was unique and utterly magnetic. I knew I wanted to invest in her friendship.

Fast forward a few years, and Susan and her family moved back to Hawaii. I found myself in Susan's lounge in the wonderful town of Kailua. As our kids played on her lanai (patio/deck), we started talking about living on this small island and what it meant for our children. As we spoke, Susan lit up like a Christmas tree and blurted out, "You have to meet Kamaile." Susan is a natural connector of people, and my answer was a big "yes."

## AUNTIES

Kamaile is a Hawaiian healer (health practitioner) whose practices are based on the traditions of her ancestry. Once I met her, there was an instant connection, just like with Susan. She had so much information on Hawaiian traditions and how Hawaiians raise children that I could hardly take it all in. We share the gift of the gab, so we spoke for a long time, going in every direction during that first meeting and during later ones. During one of our phone conversations, her four-year-old son came into the room and asked who she was talking to. She said, "It's an aunty." "Which aunty?" he asked. "Aunty Joanne," she replied. I was elated to be called aunty, an honor by any measure.

Aunties and uncles are a big part of the community. You can never have enough. They do not have to be blood relatives, just good people who share your values and become part of the village. The village helps a mother raise her children; she is not alone. She will always have people, rituals, ceremonies, and loads of aunties and uncles to lean on throughout her parenting journey. They are always there to help raise Hawaiian children and help them learn and live the Aloha Spirit. This made me think because there was a time when "doing it on your own" was a badge of honor in my parenting journey, but all it left me with was the feeling of depletion and isolation. I loved that Hawaiian mothers are encouraged to build a family of aunties around them to lean on.

## THE *AINA* (LAND)

During another conversation, Kamaile explained that one of the most important parts of raising children was teaching them to respect the land or the "*aina*." She explained, "The magic of the Hawaiian community is in the symbiotic relationship to the *aina*. Everything in nature is perfectly imperfect." With the world's environmental concerns, from global warming to plastic pollution, I felt the way she explained caring for nature was an excellent example of how to teach children to be more mindful and respectful of the environment.

Kamaile then said something I had never considered. "We are all a part of the land; we breathe the air, eat the food grown in the soil, and drink the water. How can we not see that we are a part of it?" She continued, "You have to honor where you are from. You were grown from that land, air, water, and soil." Hawaiians teach children that humans have the loudest voices of the land and should use those voices to protect it.

I left this conversation with a deeper understanding of connection. The next meal I ate with my family, I mentioned Kamaile's thoughts to my children, and we started to map out where our food came from. At the end of the day, we saw we are all part of a cycle, and now seeing this in the Hawaiian way, we will forever be mindful. If we disrespect the land on which we live, we are ultimately disrespecting ourselves.

In an era when we humans sometimes forget our connection to the earth, Hawaiian culture reminds us of its incredible importance. As the world begins to see the damaging effects of climate change, the Hawaiians, like many other native cultures (Maoris, Polynesians, Native Americans, Aboriginals, Inuits) seem to have known all along the importance of connecting with and taking care of the earth. If we continue to raise our children without an understanding and connection to the land, how bad will our planet become as we continue to disrespect its importance? It is our responsibility as parents to teach our children this incredibly valuable lesson. We cannot pass on this responsibility to our government, or Green Peace, or our children's teachers. They can help, but the responsibility lies with us. We do not have to be Hawaiian to understand the importance of taking care of our planet and the land that provides our food, air, and water. We just have to take a lesson from the Hawaiian parenting book. It is a lesson too important to neglect teaching to our children.

What values and characteristics do you want your children to have?

_____

_____

_____

_____

How can you bring the *Aloha Spirit* into your everyday life?

_____

_____

_____

_____

Make a list of five people who could become aunties and uncles to help your child grow in character and values. They will help build a village to support you and your child.

_____

_____

_____

_____

How can you better connect with the land and teach the importance of caring for the earth to your children?

_____

_____

_____

_____

## LESSONS LEARNED

- Parenting can be like the _Aloha Spirit_…focused on values and character.

- Mind and heart together.

- You can never have enough aunties and uncles.

- The importance of an extended family (the village) to help raise children.

- The importance of an extended family (the village) to support the parents.

- Teach children to respect elders.

- Connect with where you are from.

- Teach children to protect the land (earth, environment) by connecting to it.

# VALUES-BASED PARENTING

*"My doctors told me I would never walk again. My mother told me I would. I believed my mother."*

— *Wilma Rudolph, Olympian*

Wilma Rudolph's quote says it all to me. The voice of a parent has more influence on the development of a child than anything else in the world. And after seeing so many different parenting styles from so many different cultures around the world, I have come to one significant conclusion: Regardless of culture or country, parents who focus on creating a values-based approach to parenting, instead of an emotionally-based parenting approach, have closer, kinder, stronger, and more sincere relationships with their children.

Beautiful examples of values-based parenting were found in nearly every chapter of this book. In Fiji, Ice was on his hunting trip, learning about how to think about others before thinking about himself. In England, Debbie never lectured her children, but told them stories about hard life lessons. In Scotland, a B&B owner made me realize children must understand their own story to know where they came from and where they can go. In the United States, Melisa and Amy showed that working moms and stay-at-home moms both have value and do what is right for their families. And Jonathan brought in nature, biology, religion, and love into the dreaded sex talk. German families highlighted the importance of parent time and child time. Maria greeted me every morning—no matter how her day was, a greeting was her priority. My mother taught me to give freely to others through volunteering. The Hawaiians respect the land and family before anything else. And Thomas Edison's mother chose values-based parenting, following her instincts as a mother.

Every one of these stories, each from a completely different part of the world, was a values-based parenting lesson. Each lesson demonstrated a much broader perspective on parenting, focusing efforts on the essential elements in a family and children. Values.

Emotionally-based parenting can also be found everywhere you see children and parents, but understandably, it was difficult to find examples of how this was effective parenting. Emotionally-based parenting gives in to children's tantrums in the store and buys them chocolate or a toy to satisfy an immediate emotion. Emotionally-based parenting lets the number of holiday gifts determine how good the holiday is instead of how much love or tradition is given and received. Emotionally-based parenting allows the desire for one's children to always win on the sports field to get in the way of lessons learned during a losing effort. Typically, when you find parents who seem to be struggling and not enjoying their parenting journey, they are focused on emotionally-based parenting instead of values-based parenting.

I hope you have enjoyed reading these stories. I know that collecting them was an eye-opening and fulfilling experience. It taught me that being consistent in our values-based parenting, setting strong boundaries, teaching children self-respect, empathy for others, and demonstrating kindness are the most important lessons we can offer. All the stories from the previous pages offer thought-provoking ideas to help you analyze how you are parenting. I love that we are all different—how boring the world would be if we were not. I love that all children are different and grow into unique adults who will contribute to this world. I love sitting with others and learning from everyone because no two families parent the same. It is okay to follow your instincts, and it is right to give your children what you feel they need. You and your partner are the only people qualified to be your child's parent.

No matter where you are in your parenting journey, at the beginning, middle, or end (if there is ever an end), my wish is that something in this book brought goodness into your family. That was my intention. That is why I wrote this book; that is why I share, so that right now, you can take a breath and see this job we have been gifted with in a different light. Parenting is an amazing adventure.

Please contact me to let me know what you liked and how I can improve this book for the next printing. Additionally, if you are interested in a complimentary parenting consultation, please reach out to me at joanne@yourpassporttoparenting.com or find me on Facebook and/or Instagram under *Your Passport to Parenting* pages.

And with my very last paragraph, please note, if there are any grammatical errors or incoherent thoughts, this entire book was written while trying to parent two kids who kept interrupting me, asking when dinner will be ready, and where their socks are. In fact, I need to go right now, as my ten-year-old's Teddy just lost its tail and needs urgent attention—probably emergency surgery.

Sending each one of you and your families so much love and thanks.

*Joanne Holbrook*

# ABOUT THE AUTHOR

JOANNE HOLBROOK is a mother of two and spouse to a United States Army officer. She has lived and raised her family in South Africa, England, Germany, Australia, and across the United States. Born in South Africa and living nearly half her life under the controlling Apartheid Government, she yearned for a deeper understanding of cultures outside her segregated world. After seeing South Africa elect its first African President, Nelson Mandela, in 1994, Joanne began her search for cultural understanding outside of Africa when she moved to London, England.

With a Bachelor's degree in theatre and dance, Joanne performed professionally in ballet and contemporary companies for ten years in South Africa, the Middle East, and the United Kingdom. In 2002, Joanne hung up her dance shoes to follow her second passion, the theater. She worked as a production manager and then a producer with a London theater company, producing shows throughout the United Kingdom.

Joanne was soon swept off her feet (literally) by her husband Deric in 2005, when she got married and moved to Germany and then, shortly after, moved to the United States. Together, they continued indulging Joanne's desire to understand cultures in countries throughout Europe. In the United States, Joanne started a family, becoming a loving mother of two children. As an immigrant to America, and a new mother, Joanne was able to experience American cultures and gather parenting ideas from coast to coast. She lived in North Carolina, Kansas, and Washington State during her five-year stay in the United States. During this time, Joanne continued her work in dance and theater, working as a teacher and resident choreographer for ballet and contemporary companies across the country—all the while balancing a career and motherhood, which was her main priority.

With two young children under five, and after another international move back to England in 2010, Joanne's love for children with special needs drove her to begin specialized movement training for children with special needs. She began to focus her work on children who were wheelchair-bound, autistic, or had Down syndrome. In England, her parenting observations began to expand beyond culture to parents of special needs children, further broadening her views and understanding. After two years in England, Joanne and her family moved back to Germany, where she continued her work as a resident choreographer for a theater company. Ultimately winning an award for best musical choreography in Europe, she still balanced her career with motherhood, motherhood remaining her top priority.

During her next return to the United States in 2016, Joanne taught dance at the Virginia Governors School of Arts, volunteered at the Down Syndrome Association, and continued her study of movement. After experiencing a new type of parenting in America with two tweens, Joanne completed her seventh international move, this time to Australia.

It was during her Australian experience, and just before her eighth international move, this time to Hawaii, that Joanne redirected her work efforts to her original passion—understanding culture outside of South Africa, this time focusing on parenting. Joanne became an author, professional keynote speaker, parenting advocate, and entrepreneur. And through her friendships, book, and speaking events, she shared parenting stories to help build positive, values-based families around the world. What started as a desire to understand cultures outside of South Africa transformed, during motherhood and a global lifestyle, into a passion for understanding how different cultures raise their children.

Joanne currently resides in Hawaii with her husband Deric and children Kailey and Devin.

# HEARING AND SHARING MORE STORIES

I would be honored to hear how this book, or even just a few of its stories, may have helped your family. If you have any thoughts, ideas to share, or questions to ask, please email me at the address below, or find me on social media (Facebook or Instagram) at *Your Passport to Parenting*.

If you or your organization would like me to speak on the advantages of values-based parenting from around the world, I would love to meet you. I am happy to tailor a presentation or workshop to match the specific needs of your organization, group, or event.

www.YourPassportToParenting.com
joanne@yourpassporttoparenting.com